# Greenhouse gardening

## Lovell Benjamin

Pocket
Gardener

Floraprint

Published 1977 by Floraprint Limited,
Park Road, Calverton, Nottingham

Casebound edition first published 1980

Designed and produced for Floraprint by
Intercontinental Book Productions
Copyright © 1977 Intercontinental Book Productions
and Floraprint Limited

ISBN 0 903001 55 1 (casebound)

Design by Design Practitioners Limited

Photographs supplied by Floraprint Limited (copyright
I.G.A.), Humex, Halls Homes and Gardens, Harry Hebditch,
Baco Leisure Products, Harry Smith, N.H.P.A., Spectrum
Colour Library, Bernard Alfieri

Cover photograph supplied by Harry Smith

Printed in Hong Kong.

# Contents

# 1 Why grow plants under glass?

Nowadays, a greenhouse is essential for the complete gardener. One of its most important assets is that it makes possible substantial economies in household budgets: ordinary fruits and vegetables can be grown both in and out of season, and more exotic items – usually expensive in the shops – can also be produced at low cost. Seedlings and cuttings can be raised by the gardener himself, reducing annual expenditure on garden plants, and giving him the satisfaction of creating something more or less from nothing. What is more, the protection given by greenhouses against outdoor weather conditions allows many tender decorative plants to be grown, which will give enthusiasts increased pleasure.

*Right:* Greenhouse gardening provides an opportunity to grow a wide variety of colourful plants, such as the orange-flowered *Streptosolen jamesonii* shown here.

*Below:* The pendulous flowers of fuchsias provide beautiful summer flower displays in greenhouses.

# 2 Types of greenhouse

Before buying a greenhouse, look at several types and decide what sort suits your purposes best. They are usually classified according to use – and by size, shape or construction materials. The temperature and degree of humidity at which the greenhouse is to be maintained determine the type of plants which can be grown in it and also, in a general sense, the purpose for which it will be used. Experts usually refer to greenhouses in the following ways.

**Cold greenhouse** This type depends entirely on the heat of the sun for warmth, and it is therefore most valuable in the spring, summer and autumn. Its great disadvantage is that it affords little protection against severe frost and is therefore not able to protect tender plants in winter unless the season is exceptionally mild.

**Cool greenhouse** In many ways a cool greenhouse is the most useful type for most gardeners. During the summer, when unheated, it fulfils the function of a cold greenhouse. During the spring, autumn and winter it is heated enough to maintain a regular temperature of 7°C (45°F). This is sufficient to keep out the frost and so allows many tender plants to be overwintered, together with, for example, dahlias and begonia tubers. A cool greenhouse can also be used for raising plants from seed. Tomatoes given an early start in growth by greenhouse conditions will be certain to ripen no matter what sort of summer weather prevails outside.

**Intermediate or warm greenhouse** This is the type that true gardening enthusiasts, eager to extend the interest and scope of their hobby, will wish to acquire. With all the many very valuable practical aspects listed above, the warm greenhouse combines the advantage of enabling such commodities as tomatoes and cucumbers to be grown all the year round, together with some of the more exotic fruits and vegetables – such as aubergines, figs, avocado pears, peaches and nectarines. Warm greenhouses are heated to a minimum temperature of 13°C (55°F), which makes it possible to grow decorative houseplants and to carry out propagation.

**Stove or hot house** This type is more for the connoisseur than the ordinary gardener. Heated to a regular temperature of at least 18°C (65°F), it can be used for growing certain kinds of orchids; among the other plants that flourish under such conditions are aechmea, the painter's palette (*Anthurium scherzerianum*), the zebra plant (*Aphelandra squarrosa*), dieffenbachia, peperomia and strelitzia. Like the warm greenhouse, the hot house is useful for propagation, especially when a high temperature is essential.

Dieffenbachia needs a warm, humid atmosphere and so is best grown in a stove or hot house.

## Greenhouse shapes

Physically, greenhouses are classified by their shape, which to some extent determines their function. The common ones are listed below.

**Span or ridge**  This is the most popular type. It has a roof in the form of an inverted shallow V and the more conventional type has vertical glass sides, although there is now a tendency to produce this type with glass panels set at an angle of about 10° to the vertical. It is claimed that this provides greater resistance to crosswinds and a greater stability; greenhouses built in this way require less bracing, and there is better light transmission.

If mainly ground crops (such as lettuce, chrysanthemums and tomatoes) are to be grown, span greenhouses, in common with some other types, are glazed to the ground. If pot plants are to be the speciality, the glazing is usually supported on a bench-high wall of brick, concrete, wood or metal.

**Three-quarter span**  This type of greenhouse is built against a wall. It has an inverted V-shaped roof, but the span on the wall side is shorter than the other, which is of normal length. This type has an advantage over a standard lean-to (see below) in that it gives more light and headroom, but

it is more costly. One of the best uses of this greenhouse is to grow fruit on the wall side and display plants on the opposite side.

**Lean-to**  The lean-to has a single sloping roof and is built against a wall. It is the least expensive to buy and heat, and indeed, can often be heated from the domestic system. Its disadvantage is that plants grown in it tend to bend towards the light.

**Circular**  This is among the latest ideas in greenhouses. Of very attractive design, the circular type is excellent for pot plants and cultivation. However, extractor fans usually need to be installed to prevent overheating in hot weather.

*Above:* A three-quarter span greenhouse has the virtues of the lean-to type but has the advantage of giving more light and height.

*Left:* This span, or ridge, greenhouse is glazed to the base, making it valuable for growing ground crops such as chrysanthemums, lettuce and tomatoes.

*Right:* A lean-to greenhouse can be very useful, especially where space is restricted. As it is built against a wall, it is suitable for fruit.

*Above:* Both the ridge and lean-to types of miniature greenhouse are invaluable to those with little space.

*Below:* The attractive design of this circular greenhouse allows it to be positioned anywhere.

**Mini** For gardeners with only a very small space to spare, a miniature greenhouse could be the answer. Among the designs available some are free-standing, while others 'lean-to' against a wall. This type of greenhouse, though small, can fulfil many of the functions of a full-size greenhouse.

**Conservatory** This is essentially a greenhouse which is accessible from a living-room, to which it can be a pleasing adjunct. Filled with exotic plants, it makes a restful extra room in both summer and winter, combining the atmosphere of the garden with the comfort of light and heat from the domestic supply.

*Above:* A conservatory makes an excellent and very useful extension to a living-room.

## Construction materials

The merits of the various materials used in constructing greenhouses are listed below.

**Wood**   This is warm and relatively easy to work. The strongest is teak, and redwood is very popular. Both need oiling, and the latter is more easily worked. The cheaper whitewood must be regularly painted.

**Metal (steel and aluminium)**   Steel needs painting, but aluminium does not. Aluminium alloys are strong, and although light they stand firm provided the greenhouse itself is firmly sited. The metal frame must be rigid and include provision for expansion and contraction to avoid glass breakage and air leakage.

**Concrete**   Reinforced concrete is usually used for greenhouses, and although not as attractive as some other materials, concrete does provide a very durable structure.

**Downpipes and guttering**   These essentials are best made of plastic – as are water

A greenhouse constructed of red cedar requires treatment with linseed oil annually.

butts, another useful addition to the greenhouse.

**Glazing: glass v. plastic**   Glass has long proved to be a very satisfactory material for glazing, but recently plastic-glazed greenhouses have been introduced. Although not ideal, they are very cheap and functional.

The principal disadvantages of plastic as opposed to glass are:
(a) it is weathered by sun and torn by wind, and its life span is only about two years;
(b) a plastic-glazed greenhouse cools down more quickly;
(c) plastic becomes opaque and dirty because it attracts dust and cannot be satisfactorily cleaned in the way that glass can;
(d) condensation is greater: powered fans can be installed to combat it, but this will offset to some extent the saving made originally by choosing plastic instead of glass.

# 3 Choosing a greenhouse

Buying a greenhouse is an investment, so before you purchase one decide on the way you intend to use it. This, of course, depends entirely on the type of crops that are to be grown. For ground crops, such as chrysanthemums and lettuces, the greenhouse will need glazing right down to the base. Flowering pot plants and propagation call for benches, in which case the glazing can be fixed to basal walls 60–100 cm (2–3 ft) high, and heat loss will be reduced. If both types are to be cultivated, a greenhouse glazed to the ground on one side, with a bench and wall on the other, will fit the bill. With restricted space, or if wall-fruits are to be grown, a lean-to is the best proposition.

If it is the gardener's intention to cultivate plants that need heat, the most economic construction in this respect should be chosen. It is also as well to visualise the possibility of any future expansion.

## Size

Although the choice of greenhouse will depend upon the gardener's pocket, it is a great mistake to buy one that is too small.

*Above:* This greenhouse is only 2.5m (8ft) by 2m (6ft) yet has ample headroom and good space for staging.

*Left:* A greenhouse must have a door wide enough to take a wheelbarrow comfortably.

In any case, a small greenhouse is difficult to manage – it warms up too quickly in summer and cools too fast in winter. A greenhouse must have adequate headroom and, ideally, be wide enough to allow for a wheelbarrow to pass through the door. (It is important to ensure that the door opens inwards, or slides easily backwards and forwards.) Another inconvenience of too narrow a house is that it will not allow for a wide enough path, or adequate depth to the benches. A good minimum size is about 2·5 m (8 ft) wide by 2 m (6 ft) long.

# 4 Installing a greenhouse

## Siting

Careful attention should be paid to choice of location. The site should be level; if it is not, it should be levelled. It should be well-drained, sheltered from strong and cold winds and should receive plenty of sunshine. The position chosen will of course be influenced, particularly in a small garden, by miscellaneous factors such as existing paths, boundary fences, the situation of the house, etc., but the above criteria are ideal, and will also determine the direction in which the greenhouse should run. The best position is running north and south, to afford the maximum amount of light throughout the year. However, if the greenhouse is to be used largely for raising seedlings and propagating plants in winter, an east-to-west direction will give maximum light at that time of year. A lean-to should preferably be erected facing south. A conservatory is best positioned so that it forms an extension to the living room and has direct access from it.

It is also important to position the greenhouse where water, gas and electricity supplies are available, or where they can easily be made so.

**Note** Greenhouses above a certain size, stipulated by the local authority in each area, will require planning permission. Before committing yourself to buying and erecting a greenhouse, it is as well to check this point, and also to consult with neighbours regarding the proposed position of the greenhouse.

## Laying foundations and paths

A path of concrete slabs or ashes should be laid through the centre of the greenhouse. It is also advantageous to lay a path giving access from the house.

Good foundations are essential to eradicate the risk of movement, and consequent glass breakage. Solid foundations also provide good anchorage. Greenhouse makers always provide a foundation plan prior to delivery, and some also sell suitable ready-made foundations.

In aluminium greenhouses the weight to be supported is fairly low, so the foundations need not be as heavily constructed, but must still provide a firm base.

A suitable foundation for a greenhouse glazed to the ground can be provided by digging a trench 25cm (10in) deep by 30cm

*Left:* A modern conservatory with direct access from a living-room is ideal for house plants.

*Right:* Erecting a greenhouse.
(1) These two drawings show typical foundations, the first for a greenhouse glazed to the ground, the second for one with a bench-high base wall, supporting a glazed super-structure.
(2) Positioning the sides.
(3) Putting on the roof.
(4) When glazing, use putty for wood frames and plastic sealing compound for metal frames.

(1ft) wide with vertical sides. In this, a brick or concrete footing should be built. If the superstructure is to be supported on brick or concrete block walls, the top of the foundation, which in this case might be a filling of concrete, should be 15cm (6in) below ground level. Do not forget to lay the services before the concrete is put in.

## Erection

Greenhouse manufacturers always supply very complete directions for the erection of their products. The work usually consists of bolting prefabricated parts together, and calls for few tools other than spanners, screwdrivers, and perhaps a masonry drill. For glazing, use putty in a wooden greenhouse, elastic sealing compound in a metal one. Manufacturers will also erect greenhouses themselves.

## Maintenance of the fabric

The most important tasks are as follows.
(1) Occasionally treat teak and oak by wiping it with a rag dipped in linseed oil.
(2) Unless allowing it to weather, treat red cedar with a cedar preservative.
(3) Regularly paint softwood and steel. (Aluminium needs no painting.)
(4) Wash glass regularly, removing moss, etc., by scraping and hosing down.
(5) Scrub and whitewash walls annually.
(6) Paint heating pipes with aluminium paint. Do not, however, use creosote on the staging, etc., inside the greenhouse; it emits fumes which are toxic to plants.

# 5 Running a greenhouse

## Ventilation

No matter what the type of greenhouse – cold, cool, warm or stove – ventilation is most important because it enables heat and humidity to be controlled, and such disorders as 'damping off', which can have a disastrous effect, to be avoided. In a well-designed greenhouse there are ventilators, i.e. fan-lights that open, on either side of the roof, and one in each side panel. Normally, one set is provided for each 3 m (10 ft) run of length. Some greenhouses are fitted with louvre ventilators in the sides. These provide ventilation which can be very finely controlled. Ventilators on the leeward side can be opened when it is windy without there being any cold draughts. In warm weather they may be opened on both sides to reduce the temperature, control humidity and admit fresh air to the plants.

Ventilation in greenhouses demands considerable attention, and for this reason automatic methods of control have been developed. One of them is a simple device which is fitted on to each ventilator to open and shut it automatically. It does this by

virtue of a cylinder filled with a mineral substance that expands or contracts with variations in temperature. The device is very sensitive, easy to fit and comparatively inexpensive.

A second method of automatic ventilation control is to use an electic fan controlled by a thermostat. Fans are normally fitted in the gable end of the greenhouse.

*Above:* Careful attention must be paid to ventilating a greenhouse. An automatic ventilating fan, which is thermostatically controlled, can be fitted in the gable end of the greenhouse. Sometimes a fan is operated in conjunction with a louvre fitted on the outside of the mounting panel.

*Left:* An alternative method of ventilation is a mechanical system that automatically opens or shuts as necessary.

12

## Shading

Shading is another way of effectively cutting down the heat in a greenhouse, and is used in conjunction with ventilation. It is particularly valuable for certain pot plants, early propagation and tomatoes suffering from verticillium wilt. Shading can be done in the following ways.

(1) The glass on the outside can be painted with well-diluted emulsion paint, a lime and water mixture or a proprietary shading.

Such shading is effective during the summer but should be progressively washed off by winter, when all the available light is needed.

(2) Blinds, either of the venetian or the roller type, can be fitted either inside or outside; the outside type of blind is better because the sun's rays should ideally be checked before they reach the glass. There is one type of blind made from unplasticised PVC tubes, which, if they are rolled down at nightfall during winter, minimise fuel consumption in a heated greenhouse.

Shading from the hot sun is important for keeping down the temperature in a greenhouse and these external blinds made from unplasticised PVC tubes can also reduce heat loss in winter.

In some cases roller blinds fitted inside can be automatically controlled by means of a thermostat or photoelectric cell.

(3) Sun visors, in which the blinds are held rigid at the correct slope for the roof of the greenhouse, can be used. They can be controlled by an electronic eye, and are among the most efficient types of shading.

PVC blinds are excellent for shading from the sun.

# Heating

Heating a greenhouse is by no means cheap, and in the long run the final decision will depend on which fuel is cheapest and how easily a supply can be provided for the greenhouse. The choice must remain an individual one, but if, for example, the rate for the domestic gas supply is cheaper than other forms of power, then quite obviously this is the one that should be given the first consideration. The various alternatives are considered below.

**Hot-water pipes** This is the traditional method of heating a greenhouse, but it necessitates the installation of a boiler and hot-water pipes, which are usually placed under the staging. Formerly, such a boiler was fired with solid fuel, usually coke, but today gas, oil or electricity are more usual. The advantage of these is that any system

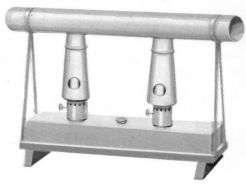

Another type of paraffin heater is the double-burner heater illustrated above.

using them can be fully automatic. Two advantages of hot-water pipes are that they distribute the heat uniformly and retain their heat for some time.

If the domestic system has enough spare capacity it may be possible to heat the greenhouse from that.

**Paraffin heaters** Although these are quite effective, the less sophisticated ones have to be regulated by hand, which can be an onerous task when temperatures are fluctuating. Paraffin heaters are good for protection during short periods of frost, but not so good for prolonged heating of greenhouses because the amount of water resulting from combustion creates heavy condensation, which in turn necessitates some form of constant ventilation. Although the relatively high carbon dioxide production from the combustion is beneficial to plants, other gases produced interfere with growth. It is also a comparatively cheap form of heating.

**Electric heaters** Although heating by electricity is costly, it has a number of advantages in greenhouses. It is clean and always reliable unless there are power cuts. With thermostats of a correct and trustworthy design, control of the greenhouse temperature can be more precise than with any other form of heating. However, once the power is cut off cooling down will take

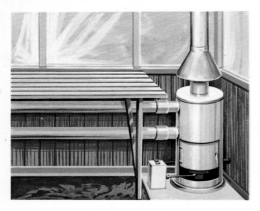

*Above:* Hot-water pipes are a long-established method of heating greenhouses.

*Left:* Paraffin heaters, such as the single-burner heater illustrated here, are useful for supplementing other sources of heat.

place, except where night storage heaters are used – but with these there are problems of temperature control, therefore they are not highly recommended.

The types of electrical equipment more usually installed for greenhouse heating are fan heaters, tubular heaters, mineral-insulated cables and soil-warming cables.

Fan heaters are extremely efficient electric heaters for a greenhouse. They are usually light, 2–2·5 kg (4–5 lbs), and are quite portable, so that they can be positioned anywhere – however, they are most usually placed in the centre of the floor. Their great asset is that they maintain a gentle movement of air, which is appreciated by plants and encourages growth. Fan heaters work on the principle of sucking in cold air at one end, warming it and blowing it out at the other one. This heated air rises naturally by convection, circulates, cools and

then falls to the ground again, where it is reheated. Fan heaters are thermostatically controlled, but even when the heating elements are switched off, the fan keeps the air gently circulating.

The great qualities of tubular heaters are their long life, almost negligible mainte-

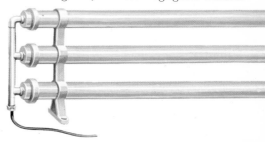

A bank of electric tubular heaters provides a clean, controllable, reliable and flexible form of heating.

nance costs, their comparatively low initial cost and their adaptability. They come in lengths ranging from 60 cm (2 ft) to 3·75 m (12 ft) with power ratings from 120 units to 720 units respectively. They are best fitted singly or in banks against the wall of the greenhouse.

Tubular heaters can, however, get very hot and scorch plants close to them unless they are thermostatically controlled. This also ensures, of course, that current is used only when necessary, and at the same time automatically maintains the required minimum temperature.

For safety reasons, it is a wise precaution to mount tubular heaters on wooden supports when installing them in a metal greenhouse.

Mineral-insulated cables are another system of heating a greenhouse. These copper-sheathed heating cables are fixed round the base wall by means of plastic brackets. They are most useful when the demand for heat is not great, and are in fact best used for protection against frost. They can be purchased in kits of different loading. Be sure to acquire a cable of the appropriate power rating for frost-protection. Cables are usually controlled

Electric fan heaters can be wall-mounted (*top*) or floor-standing (*above*). With or without thermostatic control, they are very convenient.

15

by an air thermostat, which for the latter purpose is usually set at 7°C (47°F).

Cables are usually slow to warm up – appreciably slower than warm-air fan heaters. Their surface temperature is high, and they can cause burns if touched.

Soil-warming cables are a form of local heating. This is discussed in more detail on page 19.

**Gas heaters** When burned, gas derived from coal gives off chemicals that are detrimental to plants, but the products of natural-gas combustion are beneficial, especially the carbon dioxide that enters the air. Natural-gas burning apparatus is now available for greenhouse heating. Such apparatus is easily placed below the staging and connected to the gas pipe by means of a flexible pipe. Burners can have thermostatic control and be fitted with a flame-failure device as a safety precaution.

For the running of a gas burner there must be adequate air to burn the fuel. Usually this requirement is adequately met by

A thermostat is invaluable for controlling an electrically heated greenhouse.

the normal leakage in a greenhouse. If there is any problem, an air brick in the foundation wall above ground level will solve it. Lastly, note that a gas heater may be unsuitable for a plastic greenhouse because of the condensation caused, which is heavier than that brought about by electrical heaters.

## Heat conservation

No doubt double glazing would reduce the heat losses in a greenhouse. However, the cost of hermetically sealing together two sheets of glass is high, and it would be prohibitively expensive to double glaze an ordinary domestic greenhouse.

Heat losses and draughts can, however, be reduced by lining the greenhouse inside with thin polythene, leaving the vents, of course, uncovered. Lining will increase the humidity, so careful attention to ventilation will be needed afterwards.

# 6 Fitments and equipment

## Benches and shelves

Staging is an important and valuable part of greenhouse equipment. Benches are essential when a greenhouse is to be used primarily for growing flowering pot and house plants, especially when they are displayed for their beauty. Benches are also very valuable for raising plants from seeds or rooting cuttings in boxes or pots; ideally, the benches should be slatted, to allow warm air to rise up through them from the heaters below and thus provide bottom heat. The dark place under the benches in a greenhouse with basal walls can be used for storage or for such purposes as blanching endives and forcing rhubarb.

Benches are usually fitted 75–86 cm (30–34 in) above floor level – a comfortable working height. If possible, they should be 90–105 cm (3–3½ ft) wide. Whether slatted or solid, they should be fitted away from the wall, to allow for air circulation. The materials most commonly used are wood (hard- or softwood), particularly when the

Often made of red cedar or softwood, benches or staging in a greenhouse gives more space.

benches are slatted, and aluminium. Sometimes slatted benches are supplied with timber slats and aluminium framing.

Shelves are of great value in a greenhouse, and should be of similar construction. They are very useful for keeping plants near the light, especially in winter.

Aluminium shelves, fixed above the staging to the greenhouse structure, are a great asset.

They are particularly valuable for displaying pendulous plants, such as cascade chrysanthemums. If of softwood, benches and shelves must be kept regularly painted.

## Watering

Systematic watering is essential to all kinds of plants grown in a greenhouse.

**Watering by hand** For this task it is important to have a watering-can with a fine rose that delivers a gentle stream of water, particularly when seeds, seedlings and small cuttings are being handled. The best type for this purpose is a Haws watering-can, which has a long spout with a fine rose fitted so that the perforations are almost in a horizontal plane; this ensures a gentle delivery of water.

When watering by hand it is of great value to use a moisture indicator, which takes much of the guesswork out of the task.

**Automatic watering** Watering by hand can be a hard and inconvenient chore, yet to fail to water, even once, might result in disaster. Fortunately, automatic watering systems, not too expensive and quite easy to install, are now available.

A very good type is a capillary system, which allows plants in pots to keep themselves automatically supplied with their requirements of water. The pots, which should not be crocked, are stood on a water-absorbent substance, usually sand, which is contained in a specially constructed fibreglass tray on the bench, or on a capillary fibre mat laid out on a plastic sheet directly on the staging. In either case, there is a supply trough which overhangs the front edge of the staging and is kept filled with water. The water is absorbed continuously by the absorbent substance. In the case of the sand tray, this absorption is achieved by means of a fibreglass wick partially buried in the sand with its ends in the water. The capillary mat, on the other hand, is cut to shape so that a tongue can be inserted in the trough.

With automatic watering equipment, water is transferred from a tank to the absorbent sand on which the plants are standing.

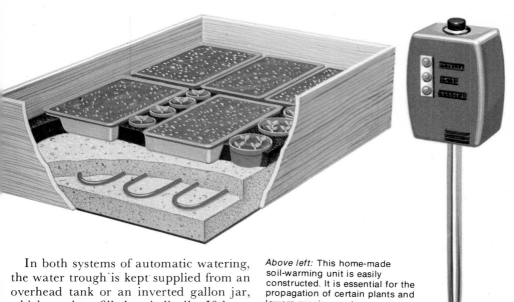

In both systems of automatic watering, the water trough is kept supplied from an overhead tank or an inverted gallon jar, which can be refilled periodically. If, however, mains water is laid on, the system can be made fully automatic by means of a ball valve and float.

## Soil warming

Soil warming is a very useful and inexpensive modern greenhouse technique. By warming the soil in the borders or on the benches, it is possible to increase the range of heat-loving plants that can be grown. It is also of the greatest use in seed germination, rooting cuttings and producing out-of-season vegetables and fruits. This can all be done without raising the temperature of the whole greenhouse.

Warming cables can be bought in lengths ranging from 6m (20ft), carrying 75 watts, which will heat $0·9–1·1$ sq m (10–12 sq ft) to 82m (267ft), carrying 1000 watts, suitable for a surface of $12·5–15$ sq m (133–166 sq ft). The soil-warming system is quite easy to install. However, if you are inexperienced in such matters, you should seek the help of a qualified electrician for connection of the cables to the mains supply. First, place a sheet of asbestos or roofing felt on the bench and erect $22·5$cm (9in) wooden walls around it. In the bottom of this enclosure, put a 5cm (2in) layer of coarse washed river sand. The warming cable is laid on this base, running evenly backwards and forwards. It is then covered with a further $5–7·5$ cm (2–3 in) of sand. The seed pans or boxes are stood on this sand. To ensure a uniform temperature throughout the bed, pack granulated peat in the spaces between the seed containers. If desired, part or the whole of the sand bed can be covered with a mixture of peat and sand and the cuttings to be rooted can be inserted directly into it.

If it is necessary to warm the air around the plants, a similar warming cable can be run round the walls, and the bed covered with a sheet of glass or plastic.

Generally, if the power is switched on for ten to twelve hours each night, all the heat needed is given. If completely automatic control is desired, a soil-warming thermostat should be fitted. Ready-wired units can be purchased.

## Propagation units

Propagation units are useful devices, particularly for rooting cuttings. To succeed in getting roots to grow on a short length of stem it is necessary to keep the stem perfectly healthy and the tissues active; if it flags in any way, rooting is not likely to take place. If, however, the process is allowed to take place in a propagation case, the temperature and humidity will be higher than if it occurs out in the open greenhouse. In consequence, the tissues of the leaves and stems remain moist and the rooting process is accelerated.

Two very simple forms of propagating case are, firstly, a seed-box covered with a sheet of glass or a polythene bag enveloping a seed pan or a pot. The more highly developed propagation units are in fact based on the elementary principle embodied in these two devices.

A propagating case has numerous uses. In the first place, it allows a cold greenhouse to be used for raising seeds and rooting cuttings with little extra expenditure on fuel. It also enables an earlier start to be made with raising seeds, which results in earlier crops in the greenhouse – for example, tomatoes. Flowers, normally produced from seeds planted during the summer for the following year, need not be exposed to severe winter weather. They can be sown in January in a propagator to produce better summer results. If a propagation unit is used in a heated greenhouse, the greenhouse can be satisfactorily run at

*Right:* This miniature propagator has dimensions of about 32·5cm (13½in) long and 20cm (8in) wide.

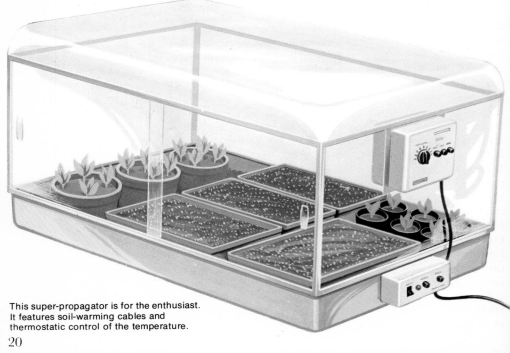

This super-propagator is for the enthusiast. It features soil-warming cables and thermostatic control of the temperature.

5–10°C (10–20°F) lower than otherwise.

Among the more sophisticated propagation cases that can be purchased, the simplest and smallest consists of a heating panel on which stands a plastic standard seed tray containing sown seeds and covered with a ventilated plastic cover. It can also be used to provide bottom heat for small pot plants and cuttings. They should be stood on *moist* gravel that almost fills the tray. There are more elaborate models, such as a multi-top unit that has four seed trays with covers, and a larger one, thermostatically controlled, with greater headroom to allow young plants to grow to maturity. This is in effect a miniature heated greenhouse that can be housed in a cooler one.

**Mist propagation**   Mention has already been made of the failure to root when a cutting dries off. While it is not a system that many amateurs are likely to employ, mist propagation is one that has been designed to lessen this risk. By this method, cuttings will root better and more quickly.

Fundamentally the equipment consists of mist nozzles which are mounted on standpipes and connected to a water-feed pipe, placed at intervals of 1–1·25 m (3–4 ft) along the bench (from which the drainage must be perfect), a control box, a solenoid valve and a detector, which is placed amongst the cuttings. The latter works on the balance principle and has two arms, one with an absorbent pad, the other being a low-voltage electrical contact. While the cuttings are being sprayed, the pad absorbs moisture and eventually becomes heavy enough to break the electrical contact of the other arm. As moisture evaporates from the pad (and the cuttings get drier), it lightens, contact is made again, and through the solenoid valve and the control box the mist is turned on. This works in conjunction with soil warming.

**Greenhouse lighting**

For the enthusiast, lighting in the

*Above:* Mist propagation is useful for rooting cuttings.

*Below:* By controlling greenhouse lighting, the gardener can make chrysanthemums bloom any time of year that he wishes.

greenhouse is essential. For general lighting, ordinary light bulbs are quite suitable; however, waterproof fittings are essential.

Another interesting aspect of greenhouse lighting is its use in extending the duration of daylight. Chrysanthemums, in particular, respond to this, because in natural conditions they form their buds during the long summer days, and flower when they shorten. By artificially lengthening and shortening the day by means of lighting, they can be made to bloom at any time.

21

# 7 Greenhouse culture

## Fertilising greenhouse plants

Greenhouse plants, like outdoor ones, need certain plant foods. The main ones are nitrogen, potassium, phosphorus, magnesium and a small number of others known as trace elements, in which iron and manganese are normally included, that are consumed in small quantities.

The functions of the main plant foods are as follows.

**Nitrogen** This element assists in leaf production, but an excess of nitrogen leads to lush growth, prone to disease. It is also an important ingredient in the synthesis of many essential plant chemicals.

**Potassium** This plays an important role in the plant's manufacture and utilisation of starch. It also assists in the development of roots, tubers, seeds and flowers, particularly enhancing the colour, and helps to ripen young wood, reducing its vulnerability to disease and early frosts.

**Phosphorus** This element plays a very important role in the formation of tissue cells and in plant growth. Without it, plants will become stunted.

**Magnesium, iron, manganese** These three are either essential ingredients of, or essential to the production of, chlorophyl, which enables plants to manufacture starch.

Greenhouse plants get their essential foods in the same way as outdoor plants – from fertiliser. The main sources of fertilisers are the composts that are used for potting, which normally contain balanced mixtures. Others are the liquid manures which are subsequently applied.

## Composts

Two growing media are used in amateur greenhouses: the traditional John Innes potting composts, and the newer soilless composts which have to a large extent superseded the former. Though most gardeners now buy their composts, it is as well to know how they are made up.

**John Innes potting composts** These are composed of loam, peat and sand, plus a fertiliser mixture (John Innes base fertiliser). The best loam for this purpose is a friable, fibrous loam prepared by allowing turves to rot in a stack. (This is becoming very hard to obtain, and hence soilless

Useful data for greenhouse gardeners:

32 litres (1 bushel) of potting compost is sufficient for:

6 standard seed boxes, 7·5cm (3in) deep

90 rooted cuttings in 7·5cm (3in) pots

50 larger plants in 11·25cm (4½in) pots

16 mature plants in 20c (8in) pots

22

composts are replacing John Innes composts.) The peat (or leaf-mould) should be sedge peat, and the sand should be washed sharp sand, graded from very fine up to 3mm (⅛in) grains.

The formula of John Innes base fertiliser is two parts (by weight) hoof and horn meal, two parts superphosphate of lime, one part sulphate of potash and one part ground chalk or limestone.

John Innes potting compost consists of a basic mixture of seven seed trays of loam, three of peat (moist) and two of sand, making two bushels (36 litres) in all. (The bushel is the traditional measure for John Innes composts.)

To this quantity is added John Innes base fertiliser in varying amounts to produce the different composts which are used as plants develop from seedlings and cuttings to mature plants.

**Soilless composts**  Soilless composts for sowing, cutting and potting are based on selected grades of peat to which have been added plant nutrients. When using them, it is important not to compact them. After six weeks, plants growing in them should be fed with liquid manure.

## Propagation

There are a number of ways in which to propagate plants. It must, however, be remembered that only with species is it possible to obtain true reproduction by sowing seeds; cultivars must be propagated vegetatively – for example, by means of cuttings.

**Seed propagation**  Most seeds will germinate readily if given some heat, ideally by placing them in a propagator.

Seeds should be sown thinly and as shallowly as possible in trays, pans or boxes. If they are very fine, mix them with sand for better distribution. Water them and place them in the propagator. Cover them with brown paper to exclude the light and close the transparent dome. As soon as germination takes place, remove the paper and lift the cover to allow the air to circulate.

When the seedlings are large enough to handle, prick them out. Use a cleft stick to lift them, and firm them into prepared holes in moist compost in another box. Shade the seedlings for a short while until they are established. Finally, when they are large enough, put each plant in a pot containing compost.

**Stem cuttings**  Different types of stem cutting are used for propagating softwoods and hardwoods. For softwood plants, nodal cuttings are usually taken. They should be about 5cm (2in) long, cut from a shoot and trimmed off with a sharp knife just below a node (leaf joint). The lower leaves should be removed. The prepared cuttings should be inserted in moist cutting compost in a box, or around the edge of a pot, and kept in a moist warm atmosphere until growth commences – evidence that roots have formed.

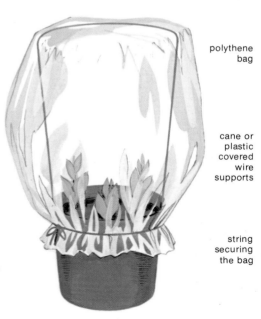

polythene bag

cane or plastic covered wire supports

string securing the bag

An improvised propagator will provide a moist, warm atmosphere for a small number of cuttings.

23

When a good root ball is formed, they should be re-potted into larger pots.

Nodal cuttings of hardwood plants are taken and prepared in much the same way, usually at the end of the growing season. They are usually about 25cm (10in) long. They should be inserted into moist compost, and should initially be shaded. When they are growing they should be potted on.

Another type of cutting, often taken from

leaf
joint
(node)

heel

plants that are more difficult to root, consists of side shoots, of about the same length, torn away from the stem with a heel of the more mature wood. This end should be inserted in moist compost and then be allowed to root.

**Stem sections**  Certain plants, such as ficus and dracaena, can be propagated by cutting a thin section of a stem containing a bud. When planted just below the surface in cutting compost a good plant will develop.

**Leaf-bud cuttings**  This form of propagation is especially suited to aphelandra, pilea, ficus and camellia. A centrally situated dormant bud is cut out from a

*Above left:* A bud cutting. The drawing on the left shows the bud being taken, and on the right it is planted.

*Top:* a nodal cutting of a softwood plant
*Above:* a heel cutting of a hardwood plant

*Below:* Crocks at the bottom of a seed box will ensure that the box has good drainage.

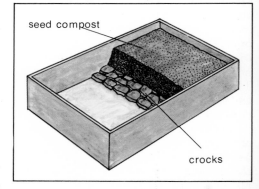

seed compost

crocks

24

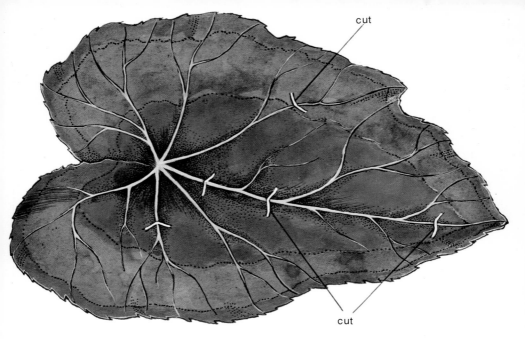

semi-ripe wood stem, with a leaf intact. The length of the portion of stem removed should be about 2cm (¾in) long. This is planted in a vertical position in cutting compost, with the leaf and bud just above the soil surface. It should be given some gentle bottom heat until the roots form.

**Division and root cuttings** Some plants can be propagated by division. This means that the root of an established plant is cut into several viable portions with a sharp knife, and planted in compost. In every case the portion used should have at least one healthy eye or shoot and some healthy roots. This form of propagation can be practised with chlorophytum, maranta, iris and dahlia. There is also another form of division, applicable to bulbs and corms. These have attached to them smaller bulbs and corms, known as offsets, which can be detached and planted in pots.

Allied to division are root cuttings. These are sections of roots cut into pieces, some 5–7·5cm (2–3in) long. They are inserted into compost in boxes, with the upper end just below the soil surface.

*Above:* Propagate fleshy-leaved plants by snipping the main veins and laying their leaves flat on compost.
*Below:* Streptocarpus are propagated by dividing a leaf and planting each part upright in compost to root.

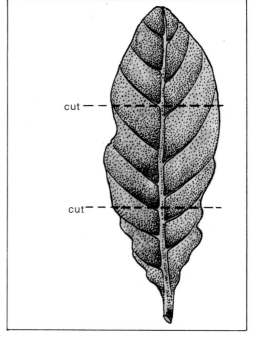

# 8 Growing vegetables under glass

The range of vegetables that can be grown in greenhouses is somewhat limited. Greenhouses do, however, provide the opportunity of raising some much appreciated out-of-season crops and the more unusual exotic vegetables which require warmer conditions. A greenhouse is also a great asset to a gardener who grows his vegetables outdoors, because it enables him to grow those seedlings which need some heat to germinate, such as celery and celeriac.

Although some vegetables will grow in pots and boxes, it is better to grow them in a border in a greenhouse glazed to the ground. In one with benches on either side, three or four tomato plants can be grown in a peat growing-bag positioned on the central path at the gable end.

## Individual greenhouse vegetables

**Aubergines** This delicious and unusual vegetable, expensive to buy, is well worth growing.

Seeds of this annual are sown in sowing compost and grown in a temperature of 18°C (65°F), preferably in a propagator, or by being placed above – for example – tubu-

lar heaters. When the seedlings have developed two leaves transplant them into 7·5 cm (3 in) pots and later 20 cm (8 in) pots, using potting compost.

Place them in a warm sunny position. To discourage red spider spray them twice daily with water. When the plants are 60cm (2ft) tall pinch out their tips and stop all side shoots two leaves ahead of the fruit.

After they have flowered encourage the fruit to set by feeding weekly with liquid manure. Keep the number of fruits down to five per plant. Harvest when the fruits are fully coloured.

Good varieties to grow are 'Early Long Purple' and 'Long Purple'.

**Lettuce** Lettuces are best grown in a greenhouse border, which should be enriched with manure or compost and the surface raked to a fine tilth. Sow the seeds successively from September to January, at three-weekly intervals, for crops from November to spring. Maintain a minimum

*Top left:* Dwarf French beans can be grown very successfully and provide very early pickings.

*Below:* Aubergines must be grown in a greenhouse or under large barn cloches.

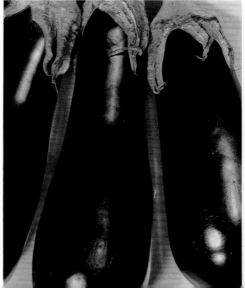

of seedlings to four. Gradually fill the pots with compost to 2·5 cm (1 in) below the top. Commence watering. As they grow, support the beans with twigs.

As the flowers begin to set, spray them daily with water – this also discourages red spider and thrips – and feed weekly with liquid manure.

Good varieties to grow are 'The Prince' and 'Masterpiece'.

**Rhubarb** Early rhubarb can be forced in a greenhouse, but it is necessary to do so in complete darkness. This can be obtained by dividing off a space under the staging using wood or asbestos sheeting, with a piece of sacking or black polythene to close the front. If the bench is slatted it should be covered with an asbestos sheet, as should any heating pipes, to prevent the soil from drying out.

*Left:* Lettuce grown as ground crops in a greenhouse provides salads throughout winter.
*Below:* Forcing rhubarb will give a winter crop.

night temperature of 7°C (45°F). The use of pelleted seeds is advantageous. Ultimately, thin them out to 22·5 cm (9 in) apart. Keep the soil moist, without wetting the leaves, and pay attention to ventilation so that the leaves are not scorched on sunny days. Spray against greenfly with malathion.

Varieties to grow are 'Kwiek' (November-December cutting), 'Kordaat' (December-February) and 'Profos' (March-April).

**Dwarf French beans** These can be successfully grown in pots or on the ground by sowing successively in October, January and February. The required temperature levels are 13°C (55°F) by day and 5°C (40°F) at night.

For the border, plant in peat pots and transplant later.

If growing beans in pots, half-fill a 20 cm (8 in) pot with moist sowing compost and sow seven seeds 2·5 cm (1 in) deep. When they are large enough, reduce the number

the seeds spaced 3·75cm (1½in) apart in sowing compost. Initially the temperature should be 21°C (70°F), and then dropped to 15° (60°F) after seven days.

When the seedlings can be handled, they should be pricked out and planted singly in 7·5cm (3in) pots, watered and shaded for a few days. When they are about 20cm (10in) tall they should be transplanted permanently into large pots filled with potting compost, or to the border. The latter needs advance preparation – by double digging, the incorporation of manure or compost, and then flooding. Some time after digging spread 132g per sq m (4oz per sq yd) of lime over the surface. At the time of planting work 132g (4oz) of fish meal into the border. Then place the seedlings in the border 45cm (18in) apart.

After transplanting, spray the plants with water twice daily for a short time. Do not saturate the roots. The plants must also be staked. As the plants grow, pinch out any shoots as they appear in the leaf axils. Assist pollination by spraying the plants with cold water each *bright, not dull*, morning (and again in the afternoon during hot weather). This makes a suitable environment for efficient pollination.

Water daily as the plants grow, and provide some shading from the direct sun. This

Tomatoes are successful greenhouse and cloche crops.

All axil shoots of tomatoes should be removed as soon as they are large enough to handle.

After frost, lift the crowns from the garden, place them in this recess on the soil or flooring, partially cover with soil and then water them. Spray lightly each day. To start with, the temperature should be 7°C (45°F) – this can be increased to 10°C (50°F) or 15°C (60°F). The sticks may be pulled when long enough.

One of the best varieties to force is 'The Sutton'.

**Tomatoes**  Tomatoes are grown preferably in a greenhouse border, or in pots or boxes on the staging when the glazing does not extend to the base of the greenhouse.

First sowings are best made in January and February in pans or seed boxes, with

**Cucumbers** Cucumbers are best sown from February onwards, according to the variety, in 7·5cm (3in) pots filled with sowing compost — putting one seed in each, pressed in on its side. Kept at a temperature of 15–19°C (60–65°F), the most robust ones, which will be growing well, will have germinated in about two days. Spray the seedlings with water and keep them shaded. When the root ball is formed, move these sturdy ones into larger pots to give their roots freedom, and throw out the weaklings. As they grow, support the stems with short canes.

In the meantime, prepare a ridge of compost 30cm (1ft) high either along the ground or on the bench, comprised of two parts turfy loam and one of strawy manure. To the above mixture add bonemeal and lime. (John Innes potting soil no. 2 is an alternative, but it loses moisture more rapidly.)

When the bed has warmed up, plant the plants firmly along the top of the ridge, 60cm (2ft) apart. Before transplanting, water the root ball in the pot. The top of the ball should protrude a little from the surface. Shade the plants from sun and maintain a temperature of 15–19°C (60–65°F).

The atmosphere must be kept humid: spray the plants twice a day and damp the bed and floor down well. Ventilate constantly to provide a good circulation of air.

Support the plants by canes at first, until they reach the horizontal wires, placed about 20cm (8in) apart, fixed to vine eyes in the glazing bars, or a specially constructed frame.

When the roots appear above the ridge, the cucumber plants should be top dressed with a mixture of soil and manure. Liquid manure should also be given.

All male flowers should be regularly removed.

Recommended varieties are 'Telegraph', 'Femdan', 'Sigmadew' and 'Conqueror'.

also helps to keep the temperature steady. Make sure there is ample ventilation.

Top-dress pot plants with compost after the second truss has formed. Feed regularly with a proprietary liquid manure, commencing with the setting of the first fruit.

If they become too tall, pinch out the tops of the plants.

Good varieties of tomato to grow include 'Ailsa Craig', 'Alicante', 'Eurocross', 'Moneymaker' and 'Supercross'.

# 9 Growing fruit under glass

A greenhouse lends itself very satisfactorily to growing both out-of-season fruit and some of the more exotic varieties that will not stand the climatic conditions outdoors. With a comparatively large greenhouse it is possible to obtain early fruit by planting both top fruit (for example, apples and pears) and soft fruit (for example, raspberries and currants) in large pots and allowing them to stand outdoors for the greater part of the year. They can be brought into shelter in February so that an early crop is obtained.

Following is a selection of fruits that are well within the scope of the amateur gardener with a relatively small greenhouse.

## Individual greenhouse fruits

**Apricots**　This fruit is best grown as a fan-trained tree, trained on wires standing about 20 cm (8 in) from the wall of a lean-to or three-quarter-span greenhouse. The soil in the border should be prepared by digging deeply and incorporating some manure or compost and a generous dose of ground chalk or limestone, or, if available, mortar (preferably lime) rubble, which also assists drainage. The soil should not be made too rich, or unnecessary growth will be encouraged.

Apricots require a cool greenhouse, with a night temperature not exceeding 7°C (45°F) in the early stages, increasing somewhat after stones have formed. Good ventilation should always be maintained.

Spray the foliage and soil with water during sunny days to maintain humidity – this also combats red spider. Cease spraying the leaves while the flowers are out and the fruits are ripening, but keep the soil damp. As the fruits swell, the tree should be given liquid manure regularly.

Apricots are pruned mainly by pinching out the young growth in the summer to induce the formation of fruiting spurs and tying in the extension growth in the sum-

Apricots only produce reliable crops in the open in warmer, sheltered districts. In other parts, they have to be cultivated in a greenhouse.

mer. Remove any unwanted wood in the autumn.

A good greenhouse variety of apricot is 'Moorpark'.

**Peaches**　Peaches are similarly grown as fan-trained trees against the wall, in soil prepared in the same way as for apricots.

They are mainly cultivated in the same way as apricots. It is, however, necessary to hand-pollinate the flowers using a camel-hair brush. When the fruits are about the size of a hazel nut, they should be thinned

30

to a distance of about 22·5 cm (9 in) apart.

The recommended day temperatures (about 3°C (5°F) lower at night) are initially 7°C (45°F), from flowering to stoning, progressively increased to 10–18°C (50–65°F), second swelling and ripening, and gradually increased to 24°C (75°F).

Fan-trained peach trees are pruned by cutting back the fruiting shoots after the fruit has been harvested to the point where a new shoot is emerging. This is then tied in. All unwanted wood is best removed in early summer.

The varieties to choose are 'Hale's Early' and 'Duke of York'.

**Strawberries** Few greenhouse gardeners can resist the temptation of a few early strawberries, which can be readily grown in pots on the bench and are easily accommodated.

Healthy plants should be planted during June and July in potting compost in clean, well-drained 7·5 cm (3 in) pots and plunged in the soil outdoors until about October, when they should be re-potted into 15 cm (6 in) pots and kept in a cold frame. In December, they should be brought inside. The starting temperature should be 10°C (50°F) rising to 15°C (60°F), with the night temperature no more than 10°C (50°F) as they come into flower. During this period the atmosphere should be kept humid by spraying on bright days.

Do not water too lavishly at first. When flowers begin to appear, water well, and feed weekly with liquid manure until the fruits begin to colour. It is advisable to hand-pollinate. Do not allow more than eight flowers to form fruit. Ventilate well, but avoid draughts. After flowering, increase the temperature a little.

A second batch can be brought in from the frame in January to provide a second crop.

Among the good varieties for greenhouse culture are 'Royal Sovereign', 'Cambridge Favourite', 'Cambridge Rival' and 'Red Gauntlet'.

*Above:* Peaches respond well to being grown in a greenhouse and are more reliable there than when they are grown out-of-doors.

*Below:* Early strawberries grown in pots give a gourmet touch to spring meals.

Most varieties of grapes will grow perfectly well in an unheated greenhouse, though many will do better with a little heating.

**Grapes** There is little doubt that grapes are the most luscious fruit that can be grown without difficulty in a greenhouse. One point that bothers many amateurs who wish to do so is the possibility that the fully developed vine might take away the light from other plants. This worry, however, can be overcome by training the growing long shoots, known as 'rods', across the north gable. This is made easier by the traditional method of planting the vine outside and training the stems through an aperture into the interior. A vine is also suitable for training on the wall of a lean-to or three-quarter-span greenhouse.

The vine should be planted firmly in January in well-drained, deeply dug soil, in which ample manure or garden compost, some bonemeal and ground chalk or lime, preferably mortar, has been incorporated. If there is more than one, they should be

placed 1–1·25m (3–4 ft) apart. The soil and atmosphere in the greenhouse should be kept moist with plenty of ventilation. Most grapes do not need heating, but better results are obtained by providing a little. There are, however, a few varieties, for example, 'Muscat of Alexandria', which need a long growing season and do best at a temperature of 10–13°C (50–55°F).

It is particularly important for grapes not to be exposed to draughts or dryness during the short time when they are about the size of a currant (the stoning period). When they begin to swell again, the fruit should be thinned using vine scissors.

Training and pruning a vine are important factors in its culture. The rods should be trained along horizontal wires fixed at intervals on the structure, set 30cm (1ft) apart, and 15cm (6in) from the glass.

The pruning programme is as follows. In the first winter, train the leading shoot as far up as possible. Cut back all laterals when they have become 60cm (2ft) long. In the second winter, prune main leader back by half or back to old wood. Cut laterals back to one bud from the point of emergence. In subsequent winters cut back all laterals to one or two buds.

During subsequent springs, on shooting, select the best growth from each fruiting spur and rub out the rest. As these shoots grow, stop them two leaves beyond the flowers. Stop all sub-laterals (the side shoots on these shoots) at one leaf along their length.

Allow fruiting to develop slowly. Remove all bunches in the first year. Allow only a few to develop in the second year after planting.

Varieties to grow are 'Black Hamburgh' (black) and 'Muscat of Alexandria' (white).

**Melons** Among the most delicious fruits that can be grown, melons can be readily produced at the time when they are expensive to buy, and are easily cultivated. Plants can be raised from seeds to crop from May onwards by successive sowing at monthly intervals from January to May. Seeds are planted 1·25cm (½in) deep, edgeways in 7·5cm (3in) pots. The seeds are germinated at a temperature of 18°C (64°F). Then the temperature needed is 16°C (61°F) and the seedlings are placed close to the glass. Pot on into 12·5cm (5in) pots.

When the plants have reached their fifth leaf, transplant them to the border, which should contain well-prepared soil enriched with manure. Alternatively they can be grown in 22·5cm (9in) pots. Each plant should have a cane inserted alongside it, up which it can be trained until it reaches the horizontal wires erected as described under 'Cucumbers', page 29.

When the main stem has reached the top wire the growing tip is pinched out, and the laterals are similarly reduced when they reach five leaves long. The flowers, male and female, develop on the sub-laterals.

During early growth, maintain good humidity by damping down the floor and spraying the leaves until the fruits reach their full size. Shade from sun, but otherwise give the plants maximum light. Artificially pollinate, preferably at midday, by removing the petals from the male flower and inserting its centre into the female.

Keep the number of fruits down to four per plant, and not more than one to a sub-lateral.

When the fruits are about 7cm (2¾in) in diameter feed with liquid manure weekly, and water copiously every morning with tepid water until they are fully grown. Because of their weight it is the practice to support the melons in nets attached to the wires.

Recommended varieties are 'Honeydew' (green-fleshed), 'Blenheim Orange' and 'King George' (orange-fleshed).

Canteloupe melons like those illustrated here can be successfully grown in a garden frame or under cloches. . Choice types like 'Honeydew' require the protection of a greenhouse in temperate climates.

# 10 Growing plants under glass

At the beginning of each of the descriptions that follow is a recommendation pertaining to the type of greenhouse needed for successful cultivation of the plant in question. Sometimes alternatives are suggested: for example, 'cool or warm'. Generally, while a specific plant can be grown under the cooler conditions, it is normally better when cultivated at the higher temperature.

### Anthurium scherzerianum
### (flamingo plant, painter's palette)

Stove. This is a most colourful plant with a bold, bright scarlet, wax-like spathe about 7·5cm (3in) wide and long, enclosing a spiral orange-red spike (spadix). Its leaves are long, shiny, lance-shaped and light green.

It is propagated by dividing the root-stock in February. The divisions are planted in potting compost in such a way that the roots are high in the pot on a slight mound. Half-fill the pot, which should be 15cm (6in) across if the size warrants it, with crocks. This plant needs humidity.

*Anthurium scherzerianum* is a colourful, fascinating and very exotic plant.

### Aphelandra squarrosa 'Louisae'
### (zebra plant)

Stove. This is a very popular, beautiful, showy plant. It has 25 cm- (10 in-)long pointed dark green leaves with veins that are boldly cream in colour. During summer and autumn it produces yellow flowers, which should be removed as they fade. Two other attractive varieties are *A. squarrosa* 'Brockfield' and *A. squarrosa* 'Silver Beauty'.

Aphelandra are propagated from cuttings taken during the spring and summer and rooted in sowing compost at 21°C (70°F) in a propagator. They should be potted on in potting compost. Feed while they are in flower.

### Aspidistra elatior
### (cast-iron plant, parlour palm)

Cool. This foliage plant was a great favourite of the Victorians and Edwardians. It has beautiful long, wide, shiny green leaves.

*Aphelandra squarrosa* is beautiful but difficult to grow.

*A. elatior* 'Variegata' has cream variegated leaves.

This plant needs little attention, although it is beneficial to sponge its leaves from time to time. It is best to re-pot it in the spring, but this should be carried out only after several years.

Propagate by dividing the rhizome in March so that each piece has some leaf and roots. Plant in potting compost.

## Begonia

Cool or warm. *Begonia rex* is grown entirely for the beauty of its leaves, which include silver, dark green, pink and darkest purple colours. It is propagated by means of the leaves, which are cut across the back of the main veins and pinned down flat on a surface of cutting compost in a tray. They are then placed in a propagator at 18–21°C (64–70°F). Another interesting foliage begonia is *B. masoniana* (iron cross begonia).

*B. semperflorens* is fibrous-rooted and has red, pink or white flowers; these begonias make lovely greenhouse plants for the later autumn. Seeds are sown in late June. They should be put into a propagator at 18°C (64°F) and then potted on. They like humid conditions.

Begonia 'Gloire de Lorraine' (Christmas begonia) is winter-flowering, with clusters

*Aspidistra elatior* 'Variegata' is grown for its foliage.

of delicate rose-pink flowers. It is propagated from cuttings and basal shoots taken in spring and ultimately potted on in 15 cm (6 in) pots. It likes a moist and semi-shady warm position when potted. Its stems must be supported. Remove all flower buds until October, when they should be allowed to develop, and then give weekly doses of liquid manure. After flowering, cut the plants down by half and keep them, watering little, until early spring when they will provide more cuttings.

## Beloperone guttata
## (shrimp plant)

Warm. This plant's common name results from its pinkish-brown bracts that resemble shrimps. It prefers a warm house and should be grown in well-drained potting compost. It should be given plenty of water during the summer, but little in the winter.

Cuttings should be taken in early summer and inserted in soilless sowing compost

Few greenhouse plants are more beautiful than *Begonia rex*, with its colourful, almost triangular leaves.

35

*Beloperone guttata* has become a favourite exotic pot plant. It seldom exceeds 30cm (1 ft) in height.

at 18°C (64°F), and then potted on into 7·5cm (3in) pots and afterwards 13cm (5in) pots. Bushiness should be induced by regular pinching back of the shoots. When established, give liquid manure regularly during the summer.

## Bouvardia x domestica

Warm. Nowadays it is usual to grow varieties, of which 'President Cleveland, with its terminal clusters of bright crimson-scarlet tubular flowers, is representative. They flower from August to September.

After flowering, rest the plants with little watering until late February. Then water the soil and spray the stems to start fresh growth. Also prune, if necessary. Pinch back during the summer to encourage late flowering.

Propagate from cuttings from young shoots placed in a propagator at 19°C (66°F), or from root cuttings.

## Brunfelsia calycina (Franciscea calycina)

Stove. Has fragrant, salvia-shaped violet-purple flowers with a long tube, which fade to almost white from April to August. The variety 'Macrantha' has 7·5cm (3in) wide flowers.

After flowering, shorten the stalks by half and encourage new growth by spraying with water. Provide a moist atmosphere.

Propagate from cuttings taken between February and August. Insert in soilless cutting compost and give bottom heat at about 21°C (70°F).

## Bulbs (spring)

Most bulbs are easy to grow, and do not need any great heat. They provide a magnificent display in the greenhouse. A few planted successively from late summer onwards will bloom from Christmas until May. As they spend much of their growing time in plunge beds outdoors, they do not

36

take up space in the greenhouse for long.

The most popular bulbs are daffodils, narcissi, hyacinths and tulips. Daffodils, hyacinths and narcissi should be planted so that their noses are just visible through the surface of the soil, tulips should be just covered, and small bulbs such as crocuses and snowdrops buried by 6–12mm (¼–½in).

The following description of the cultivation of narcissi bulbs is fairly typical, despite small modifications for other bulbs.

Narcissi bulbs should be planted in John Innes potting compost no. 2 or a soilless potting mixture. A 15cm (6in) pot will accommodate three or four bulbs.

After planting, place the pot in the soil in a cool plunge bed outdoors for about eight weeks, when the young, pale green leaves appear. Then bring them into the greenhouse and stand them in a dim light until

Trumpet daffodils brighten the dark days of winter.

the leaves turn green, when the pot should be given more light and warmth – a day temperature of 10°C (50°F) – until the plants flower. Water and feed with liquid manure about every three weeks.

After it has flowered, put the plant outside. When the leaves are dead, harvest and dry the bulbs, and use them *outdoors* the following year.

Narcissi bulbs which are planted in August or September will flower from December to January.

Daffodil bulbs planted in August-October flower from January to April.

Tulip bulbs planted in September-October flower from January to April. These will stand rather more heat, up to 15°C (60°F).

Hyacinth bulbs planted in September-October flower from January to March. These usually take about seven weeks to produce growth when plunged.

Calceolaria are best grown in pots under glass.

### Calceolaria
### (slipper flower)
Cool. It is the herbaceous calceolaria that is grown most frequently in a greenhouse. This has large clusters of red-orange and red flowers with distinctive markings and ovate mid-green leaves. Many fine hybrids are obtainable.

The seeds are sown thinly in seed compost and germinated at 18°C(64°F) during June, with shading when needed. Prick off the seedlings singly into pots in July and keep in a cold frame. In September pot on into 10cm (4in) pots and take inside. Keep warm and moist at night at a steady temperature. In February pot on again in 20cm (8in) pots using growing compost. Keep near the glass, shading from strong sun. Stake securely and water modestly. Feed with liquid manure fortnightly when buds appear.

## Camellia

Cool. These popular plants are much appreciated for their shapely white, pink and red flowers and their rich green, shiny, bold foliage. They need comparatively little attention other than regular, fairly modest watering and occasional feeding. They might need re-potting every three or four years.

They can be propagated by taking leaf bud cuttings.

## Campanula isophylla
## (bellflower)

Cool. *Campanula isophylla* is a prostrate plant, which overhangs the rim of its pot and has star-shaped blue flowers in abundance during August and September. Its cultivar *Campanula isophylla* 'Alba', with white blooms, is even more charming. It is useful for hanging baskets.

It should be watered and fed regularly while flowering and dead-headed regularly. Keep comparatively dry in winter.

Propagate from cuttings from sturdy basal shoots taken in spring. Insert these in cutting compost and provide some warmth.

## Carnations

Cool. Carnations will produce flowers continuously throughout the year, with some peak periods, in a cool, well-ventilated greenhouse with plenty of headroom.

New carnations are usually supplied in spring in 7·5cm (3in) pots. On arrival they

*Campanula isophylla* is excellent for a hanging basket.

can be transplanted into 15cm (6in) pots, or to a raised (22·5cm- (9in-)high) bed on the ground, of either John Innes potting compost no. 4 or a soilless compost. Place the plants 20cm (8in) apart each way in the bed.

When the plants are growing well, pinch their tips out to encourage the growth of side-shoots. When these are about 15cm (6in) long, they in turn can have all the buds removed, except one, so that each stem only bears one good bloom.

Regular watering is very important: water quite copiously during the summer, with much less in winter when growth slows up. A night temperature of up to 10°C (50°F) is suitable; during the summer a little light shading might be needed to lower the daytime temperature.

Carnations should be supported with canes and wire rings when in pots, and with large-mesh netting, about 15cm (6in), strung from four corner posts when growing in a bed. After the first blooms are cut, the carnations should then be fed with a fertiliser which is suitable for carnations.

Carnations last two years, so new stocks should be raised by taking side cuttings in early spring. Plant them in cutting compost and place them in a propagator at 16–18°C (61–64°F), admitting air when the tips begin to grow and lowering the temperature to 10°C (50°F) over the course of a week. Then pot into 7·5cm (3in) pots. When they are 22·5cm (9in) tall, remove the growing tip; repeat if desired when the resultant side shoots are long enough. Pot on when needed.

## Chlorophytum (spider plant)

Cool or warm. *Chlorophytum elatum* 'Variegatum' is the variety most grown, solely for its long, grass-like leaves, which are green with a broad streak of white running down their centre. These plants are excellent for hanging baskets.

The spider plant is very easy to grow. Apart from reasonable watering during the summer, and a regular feed with liquid manure, little more is needed.

Inconspicuous flowers develop in the ends of long slender stems, weighing them down. Chlorophytum can be propagated by planting the plantlets that are formed as the flowers fade. Otherwise, root divisions can be taken in spring or summer.

## Chrysanthemum (late-flowering)

Cool. Start with disease-free, rooted cuttings. Subsequently new plants can be raised by taking cuttings from the old plants.

To do this, cut selected healthy plants down to 15–22·5cm (6–9in) *immediately* after flowering, still keeping them in their pots. Give them an initial watering, and

keep them in a light airy position in the greenhouse at a temperature no higher than 10°C (50°F) without much further watering.

After a time basal shoots will appear. Choose healthy shoots about 3 mm (⅛ in) thick, with four or five fresh leaves closely spaced along the stem, for cuttings. Guard

*Chlorophytum elatum* 'Variegatum' (spider plant) is very easy to grow and propagate.

against greenfly by spraying them with malathion. Propagate by cutting the shoots just below a node.

If necessary, trim off any lower leaves to facilitate planting. Wet the lower ends of the stems and insert in a rooting compound. Shake off the surplus powder, and insert in John Innes potting compost no. 1 or soilless cutting compost, 5cm (2in) apart, in a seed-box. Place the cuttings in a moist atmosphere and provide bottom heat up to about 15°C (60°F) for about a week or ten days, preferably in a propagator. When they show signs of growth shade them with paper on bright days, and when they become robust give the cuttings both ventilation and a temperature which is no higher than 7°C (45°F).

When they are well rooted, transplant the cuttings into John Innes potting compost no. 2 or soilless potting compost in 7·5cm (3in) pots and place them in a cold frame. About the end of May, when the root ball is well-formed, pot on into John Innes potting compost no. 4 or soilless potting compost in 22·5 cm (9 in) pots. At the same time, insert two stakes, at least 1m (3ft) tall, in the compost either side of the plant. Tie each stem securely but not tightly to these.

Stand the potted chrysanthemums outdoors in rows on boards or another hard surface for the summer. To prevent them from blowing over, tie the stakes to horizontal wires running along the rows. In late September bring the pots into the greenhouse, giving them good ventilation and a little heat.

Chrysanthemums first form a terminal bud on the main stem. As soon as the side shoots appear at the leaf joints, remove this bud, for it will either die or give poor flowers. Allow the side shoots to develop buds. The centre large one, known as the first crown bud, produces the best decorative blooms. All the other buds on each side shoot that is retained should be removed,

*Clivia miniata* blooms best when it is pot-bound. It is as tough and durable as the aspidistra.

leaving one bloom to a stem. All further side shoots should also be pinched out as they form.

## Clivia miniata

Cool. This plant has strap-shaped leaves and lily-like clusters of flowers of orange-

Chrysanthemums are first 'stopped' by pinching out the 'break bud', which either dies or flowers poorly, appearing on the main stem when shoots first appear in the leaf axils (*left*). The latter are eventually 'disbudded' to leave the centre bud or 'first crown bud', which produces the best blooms. It is then 'secured' by removing any further axil shoots that appear (*right*).

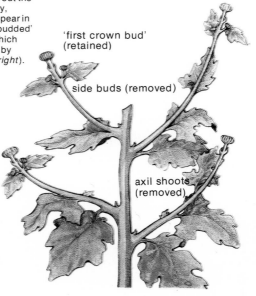

'break bud' (pinch out)

main stem

side (axil) shoots

'first crown bud' (retained)

side buds (removed)

axil shoots (removed)

red. Young plants need re-potting every year into 20cm (8in) pots. Mature plants may remain undisturbed for several years if they are top-dressed with fresh rich soil annually, and fed occasionally with liquid manure. After they have flowered keep them warm and moist. Then give them a resting period, which can be induced by minimising watering.

Propagation is best achieved by division after flowering or from offsets.

## Codiaeum
### (croton)

Stove. Various crotons are grown for their leaves, variegated with brilliant hues ranging from yellow to orange-pink, red and crimson. These colours are more vivid in plants raised annually.

The plants need a moist, very warm atmosphere all the time and must have good light. They should be well watered during the summer and given a weekly feed of liquid manure. They are best potted on annually in spring.

They can be propagated by cuttings at any time from the ends of shoots, inserted singly in 5cm (2in) pots of cutting compost and put into a propagator at 21°C (70°F).

Good crotons to grow are *Codiaeum variegatum pictum* and its cultivars 'Carrierei', 'Disraeli' and 'Reidii'.

## Coleus blumei

Cool or warm. Coleus are grown for their colourful foliage. They should be regularly watered during the summer, and much less so in winter. A temperature of 13°C (55°F) is best in winter. Feed with liquid manure weekly from June to September. Growing

*Codiaeum variegatum pictum* (croton) is extremely rewarding but is not really easy to grow.

tips should be pinched out to encourage bushiness.

Seeds may be sown in February and germinated at 16°C (1°F). When large enough, pot the seedlings on into 7·5cm (3in) and then 13cm (5in) pots. Alternatively, take tip cuttings of non-flowering shoots in spring. Plant them in cutting compost in 7·5cm (3in) pots and keep them in a temperature of 16–18°C (61–64°F).

*Columnea gloriosa* is a beautiful trailer. Though not the easiest to grow, it is well worth persevering with it.

## Columnea gloriosa

Stove. With its tubular flowers of bright scarlet and drooping habit, *Columnea gloriosa* is ideal for hanging baskets. It flowers during the winter.

It needs a warm, humid atmosphere (no lower than 13–16°C (55–61°F) during winter). Feed established plants regularly with weak liquid manure during the summer. Re-pot this plant every other year in June.

Pieces of stems root quite easily in a cutting compost placed in a propagator with a temperature of 18–21°C (64–70°F) and a humid atmosphere. The stem pieces should be taken in spring.

## Cyclamen persica

Cool or warm. The modern strains of the Persian cyclamen, a popular winter-flowering plant, have blooms in shades of purple, red, pink, mauve and white and combinations of these, and variously silver-marbled leaves.

The plants should be brought into the greenhouse in September and given ample ventilation, light and a temperature of 10°C (50°F). Watering must be done carefully from the bottom without wetting the bare corms. After flowering, the plants should be rested by gradually watering less and, during the summer, laying the pots on their sides to dry off. In autumn, growth should be re-started by watering.

Cyclamen are best propagated from seeds sown in August at a temperature of 13–16°C (55–61°F). Then pot them on until they are in 13cm (5in) pots. At no stage should the corms be buried.

## Dieffenbachia picta
## (dumb cane)

Stove. This has dark green, pointed, oblong leaves covered with white and pale green spots. Its cultivar 'Rudolph Roehrsii' is mottled pale and dark green.

Dieffenbachia needs a humid atmosphere with a winter temperature not lower than 16°C (61°F).

It is propagated from suckers or stem sections containing an eye in a cutting compost at a temperature of 21–24°C (70–75°F) in a propagator.

## Dracaena draco
## (dragon plant)

The species and varieties of dracaenas are grown for their superb range of foliage. Among the more attractive species are the smaller *Dracaena godseffiana* and *D. sanderiana*. A larger cultivar is *D. deremensis* 'Warneckii', which has long grey-green leaves with two silver stripes.

The plants need a winter temperature of 10–13°C (50–55°F), rising to 16°C (61°F) at night in spring and summer to encourage

42

*Dracaena fragrans* 'Massangena' has attractive green and gold leaves and likes a warm, humid atmosphere.

growth. The atmosphere must be humid.

They are propagated from cuttings of a main stem, partially buried horizontally in cutting compost in a propagator at 21–24°C (70–75°F).

### Euphorbia pulcherrima (poinsettia)

Warm or stove. This splendid plant has insignificant flowers, but large scarlet, leaf-like bracts in winter. It is also available in pink and cream forms.

It needs a winter temperature of 13–16°C (55–61°F). During the summer it needs a humid atmosphere. It should be watered freely while growing, but after flowering it should be kept just moist. Give weak liquid manure weekly from June to September, during which period it can stand outdoors.

Poinsettia is difficult to preserve from one season to another so it is better to grow new plants from cuttings taken in spring. These should be inserted singly in 7·5 cm (3 in) pots of cutting compost and placed in a propagator at 18–21°C (64–70°F). The rooted cuttings should be potted on, and feeding should begin in their final pots.

### Ficus elastica 'Decora' (india-rubber plant)

Warm. This plant is grown for its rich, green, bold foliage.

In winter it needs a temperature of 16–18°C (61–64°F). Water freely in summer and keep just moist in winter. Place in a well-lit position, but out of direct sunlight. Provide a humid atmosphere in summer, with ventilation when needed, and pot on every other spring. Feed with weak liquid manure during the summer.

The plant can be propagated from cuttings of lateral shoots taken from April to June at a temperature of 21–24°C (70–75°F), or from leaf-bud cuttings.

Few plants can surpass *Euphorbia pulcherrima* (poinsettia) for the splendid colour it gives.

There are many beautiful varieties of indoor fuchsia, which are grown as both bushes and standards.

## Fuchsia

Cool or warm. The tender varieties of fuchsia are attractive as pot plants and provide beautiful summer flower displays in greenhouses.

After resting during winter, when they should be kept in a dry, well-lit place at a temperature of 4–7°C (39–45°F), fuchsias should be started into growth by being plunged into water and kept at a temperature of 10°C (50°F). (Any cuttings required should be taken when the young growth appears.) After removing as much soil as possible from the roots, pot the plants in John Innes potting compost no. 3 in a similar or smaller pot.

During the spring and summer fuchsias should be allowed to stand in a cool, well-lit place out of direct sunlight. Real success with fuchsias results from feeding and watering well during the growing and flowering season. Spraying the foliage with water occasionally is also advantageous.

Cuttings should be taken from shoots with no flower buds and should be nodal. They should be inserted in 5 cm (2 in) pots of cutting compost and placed in a prop-

agator at 16°C (61°F) until they are rooted, when air should be allowed in and the temperature lowered to 10°C (50°F). Young plants destined to be bushes must have their growing tip pinched back to induce bushiness. This may be repeated once or twice more if necessary. For standards, the plants should not be pinched back, but the main stem should be allowed to grow, removing all laterals as they appear, until the required height is reached, when it should be stopped.

Fuchsia bushes should be pruned lightly in February. At this time, overgrown plants can be hard-pruned to reduce their size. Standards are also pruned.

Pendulous varieties, such as 'Falling Stars' and golden-foliaged 'Golden Marinka', are excellent for hanging baskets, either to beautify a greenhouse, or to hang outdoors during the summer.

## Gerbera
## (Transvaal daisy, Barberton daisy)

Cool. *Gerbera jamesonii* has orange-scarlet, daisy-like flowers from May to August. There are also many hybrids and varieties in a wide range of colours.

Gerbera needs well-drained soil and cool conditions, with a temperature of 5–7°C (41–45°F) during the winter. Water freely in summer and more sparingly in winter, ventilate well and provide some shade when necessary. Apply weak liquid manure at fortnightly intervals during the summer.

Gerbera can be propagated by division in March. Alternatively, sow seeds in seed compost in February at a temperature of 16–18°C (61–64°F). Prick out and pot on in the usual manner.

## Grevillea robusta
## (silk bark oak)

Cool. *Grevillea robusta* is a foliage shrub with pinnate leaves up to 37·5 cm (15 in) long.

It requires a winter temperature of 4–7°C (39–45°F) and can be stood out of doors from May to October. Water freely in spring and summer and keep just moist

*Above: Grevillea robusta is beautiful and easy-to-grow.*

*Below right: Hoya carnosa is relatively unknown.*

during winter. Feed fortnightly with liquid manure during summer. Re-pot in March every two years, increasing the pot size if necessary.

This plant is propagated from seed sown in March in pots of lime-free sowing compost and germinated at 13–16°C (55–61°F). Prick out into 7·5cm (3in) pots and then pot on as necessary.

## Hippeastrum
### (amaryllis)

Warm or stove. Hippeastrum are showy, bulbous plants with strap-like green leaves and blooms of white, pink, red or orange, sometimes striped or frilled, according to the hybrid.

Plant one bulb in a 15cm (6in) pot of growing compost with half the bulb exposed and water sparsely until growth begins. As soon as the flower bud appears, or shortly afterwards, water freely and feed weekly with liquid manure. Maintain at a minimum temperature of 13–16°C (55–61°F). When leaves turn yellow, keep dry until re-starting growth in autumn.

Propagate from offsets or seeds sown in the springtime.

## Hoya carnosa
### (porcelain flower)

Cool or warm. This is a climber with deep green, glossy leaves and clusters of pale pink, sweetly scented flowers during summer.

Keep *H. carnosa* at 10°C (50°F) in winter and at not less than 16°C (61°F) in spring and summer. Provide a little shade when necessary, and abundant water, except in winter. Maintain a good level of humidity in spring and summer and also spray the plant with water when hot. Give liquid manure every three weeks in summer.

The plant is propagated by cuttings 7·5cm (3in) long taken in June and July. Root at 16–18°C (61–64°F) in a propagator.

## Impatiens sultanii
### (busy lizzie)

Cool or warm. Busy lizzie has white, orange, magenta, crimson or scarlet flowers from April to October.

It needs a winter temperature of 13°C

(55°F). When growth re-starts in March, water fairly freely. Liquid-feed weekly from May to September and provide a little shade on hot days. Re-pot every other year in April.

Propagate from tip cuttings inserted in cutting compost at any time from April to May. Place in a propagator at 16°C (61°F).

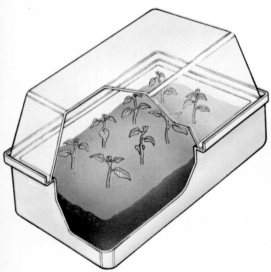

*Above: Impatiens sultanii can be propagated from tip cuttings in a simple propagating unit given bottom heat.*

*Right: Maranta leuconeura 'Kerchoveana' is called the 'prayer plant' because it raises its leaves at sundown.*

## Jasminum mesneyi (syn. primulinum) and J. polyanthum

Cool. *Jasminum mesneyi* (syn. *primulinum*) has yellow flowers in spring. *J. polyanthum* has white and pale pink blooms in winter. Both are climbers.

Both do best in a greenhouse border, but they can be grown in 30 cm (12 in) pots. They should be trained up wires. In winter, a satisfactory temperature is 10–13°C (50–55°F). Keep the compost moist continuously and water freely during the growing season.

Propagate from heel cuttings and give bottom heat of 16°C (61°F).

## Maranta

Stove. These are ornamental foliage plants, with leaves of various shapes marked or streaked in vivid colours. The two most strikingly coloured plants are *Maranta leuconeura* 'Kerchoveana' and *M. L eryth-rophylla*.

They need a winter temperature of 13°C (55°F), ample watering in summer, more moderate watering in winter, a humid atmosphere, a daily spraying and a fortnightly liquid feed during their growing season.

They are propagated by rhizome division in April or by planting basal shoot cuttings in the summer in cutting compost at 21°C (70°F).

## Palms

Cool. Small palms make good table decorations, and the larger specimens are most attractive for the greenhouse and conservatory. Amongst the most excellent is *Chamaedorea* (syn. *Neanthe*) *elegans* 'Bella' (parlour palm), with elegant pinnate leaves, up to 1·25m (4ft) long, that hang down gracefully. It should be watered

*Above:* Groups of *Howea belmoreana* can have a striking decorative effect.

*Left: Neanthe elegans* is a perfect palm to grow because it requires so little attention.

freely in summer and have its leaves sprayed weekly. Feed throughout the growing season. Give partial shade: too much sun turns the foliage brown. It needs re-potting only when it becomes pot-bound, and this is rare.

*Howea* (formerly *Kentia*) *belmoreana* (curly palm) is a palm with dark green pinnate leaves 45 cm (18 in) long and 30 cm (12 in) wide, carried on 45 cm- (18 in-)long stems.

*Howea* (formerly *Kentia*) *forsteriana* (Kentia palm), another excellent species, has leaves that differ from those of *H. belmoreana* only in that they droop and have fewer leaflets.

Both of these are grown in a growing compost. Ideally, they should be given a winter greenhouse temperature of 10–12°C (50–54°F); the minimum should be 7°C (45°F). *Howea* need full light in winter, with

some shading in summer. Water sparingly between November and March, abundantly from April to July and moderately between July and October.

All the above-mentioned palms can be propagated from seed. Place the seed on the surface of some peat in a seed-pan, and germinate at a temperature of 27°C (81°F). Transplant the seedlings to 7·5cm (3in) pots of growing compost and maintain a temperature of 18°C (64°F) until they are growing.

## Pelargonium

Cool or warm. Fuchsias and pelargoniums have a number of common uses, including greenhouse display, hanging baskets, indoor pot plants and summer bedding.

Among the pelargoniums there are two outstanding groups of hybrids – the regal pelargoniums, among which there are some very beautiful named varieties, such as 'Black Knight', 'Lavender Grand Slam', 'Carisbrooke' and 'Nomad', and the zonal pelargoniums. These latter are commonly known as geraniums, and include several outstanding named cultivars (such as 'Cleopatra', 'Du Barry' and 'Gustav Emich'), varieties of the Irene seed strain, which is regarded as one of the best (such as 'Electra', 'King of Denmark' and 'Maximum Kovaleski') and varieties of foliage geraniums, both pendulous types and miniature ones suitable for hanging baskets.

Although pelargoniums can be maintained in a greenhouse from year to year, it is more common to take cuttings annually.

Nodal cuttings are taken in August and inserted individually in 7·5cm (3in) pots of John Innes potting compost no. 1, or in soilless sowing compost. Keep them covered with paper from seven to ten days. Normally no heat is required for rooting. Pinch out the growing tips to form good bushes when the plants are about 15cm (6in) high. Pot on into 10–15cm (4–6in) pots. Maintain a winter temperature of 7–10°C (45–50°F) and keep the soil just

*Above:* Pelargoniums are among the most popular and colourful plants to cultivate in a greenhouse.
*Left:* Zonal pelargoniums are available in many colourful varieties, all of which are most attractive.

moist. Water freely during the growing season. Keep the greenhouse well-ventilated and provide shade during the hottest weather – do not let the temperature exceed 13°C (55°F). When well-rooted feed with liquid manure until the flowers open.

## Peperomia

Stove. These are mostly moderate-sized or small plants. They like shade from the sun, and grow in well-drained compost. They should have a humid atmosphere during summer and be sprayed twice daily, but they must not be overwatered and be allowed to dry out before the next watering. The best winter temperature for them is

13–18°C (55–65°F) and in summer 15–24°C (60–75°F).

They are propagated by cuttings inserted singly in 5 cm (2 in) pots of cutting compost in a propagator at 24°C (75°F).

## Pilea

Stove. Of these attractive foliage plants, *Pilea cadierei* (aluminium plant) and *P. muscosa* (artillery plant) are the best known.

They require a winter temperature of 13°C (55°F) and a summer one of 24°C (75°F). They also need full light in winter and moderate shade in spring and summer. Water freely from April to September, very moderately in winter. Feed fortnightly during summer.

Propagate from cuttings in May. Insert in cutting compost and place in the propagator at 18–21°C (64–70°F).

## Plumbago capensis

Cool or warm. This is a lovely deciduous climber with panicles of blue flowers from April to November.

While it can be grown in a pot, it is best planted in the border and trained up wires or a trellis. It should be watered well until after flowering, and then kept just moist and watered increasingly as new growth

*Pilea cadierei* is a very charming foliage plant.

appears. The best temperature up to December is 13–16°C (55–61°F); the minimum during the winter is 7°C (45°F). Feed regularly during the summer and re-pot annually in the spring.

Propagate from heel cuttings at a temperature of 16–18°C (61–64°F).

## Primula

Cool. Primulas are excellent for greenhouses. There are many species, but possibly the most popular for growing under glass are *Primula malacoides*, *P. sinensis*, *P. obconica* and *P. x kewensis*.

*P. malacoides*, although a perennial, is usually grown as an annual. Its leaves are hairy, ovate and pale green. Whorls of star-like flowers, ranging from pale lilac-purple through to red to white in colour, open between December and April.

*P. sinensis* is also a perennial grown as an annual. Its thick stems bear two or three whorls of pink, lilac or white flowers during winter.

*P. obconica* is also grown as an annual. Its light green leaves cause a rash on sensitive skins. Its winter-produced flowers are in

*Peperomia caperata* has curious cream flowers, like shepherd's crooks, borne on light brown stalks.

clusters of pink, red, lilac or blue-purple.

*P. x kewensis*, a perennial hybrid, has fragrant, yellow flowers, borne in whorls on upright stems during the winter.

All primulas require a minimum winter temperature of 7°C (45°F). Always keep the plant moist. Feed weekly with liquid manure when the flower stalks start to lengthen.

All are propagated from seeds at 16°C (61°F). Prick off the seedlings into boxes, and transplant them singly into 7·5cm (3in) pots of growing compost. Plunge them outdoors in a shaded frame for the summer. In autumn, pot them on to 15cm (6in) pots.

A very beautiful plant, *Primula obconica* must be handled with care, as its leaves affect sensitive skin.

*Rhododendron* (syn. *Azalea*) *indicum* is a lovely plant for Christmas decoration.

## Rhododendron (syn. Azalea) indicum (Indoor or Indian azalea)

Cool or warm. This is an evergreen with many varieties which become massed in red, pink or white flowers during the winter or early spring.

In autumn the plant should be stood in a well-lighted place and sprayed with clear water. The compost should be kept moist, but not over-wet. An occasional feed with liquid manure helps to swell the buds.

After it has flowered, remove the dead flowers and put outdoors in the sun after the danger of frost has passed. During the summer keep the plant in the shade, water and feed until early October and then bring it back under the glass. If necessary, re-pot into a larger pot after flowering.

Propagate from half-ripened cuttings taken in April, inserted in cutting compost with a little bottom heat. They are not easy to root. Rooting compounds and mist propagation will be helpful, however.

## Saintpaulia (African violet)

Warm. A charming small plant with pleasant fleshy green leaves and violet-like flowers, mainly pink and purple in colour.

*Saintpaulia ionantha*, the species normally cultivated, needs a winter temperature of 13°C (55°F). The atmosphere should be humid. Always keep the soil moist, without wetting the plant's leaves. Feed fortnightly with liquid manure during the summer.

Propagate from leaf cuttings during the summer. Place in a propagator at 18–21°C (64–70°F). It may also be grown from seed, germinated at the same temperature.

### Sanseviera trifasciata 'Laurentii' (snake plant, mother-in-law's tongue)

Warm or stove. *Sanseviera trifasciata* is essentially a foliage plant, with narrow, fleshy, pointed and slightly twisted leaves edged with yellow and banded with light and dark green.

Minimum winter temperature should be 10°C (50°F). Allow the plant to dry out in the summer between waterings. Feed monthly from May to September.

Propagate from suckers potted up in growing compost.

*Below:* Saintpaulia is among the most spectacular of plants that can be grown in a greenhouse.

*Sansevieria trifasciata* 'Laurentii' is nicknamed Mother-in-Law's Tongue.

## Senecio (syn. Cineraria) cruenta

Cool. There are numerous varieties which form compact masses of daisy-like flowers from December to May, according to when they were sown, in colours which include white, lavender, blue, mauve, red, pink and various bicolours.

Plant in John Innes potting compost no. 2 or soilless growing compost, and keep them at a temperature of 8°C (46°F) from October onwards, during which period the plants should be fed fortnightly with liquid manure and watered – but not over-watered – regularly.

They can be raised from seed between April and August at a temperature of 13°C (55°F). Grow the seedlings on through the summer in 7·5cm (3in) pots in an open frame, shading with muslin during hot spells; bring them into the greenhouse in September.

*Sinningia speciosa* (Gloxinia) is essentially a greenhouse plant, with large bell-like flowers.

## Sinningia speciosa (Gloxinia)

Cool or warm. Gloxinias have large bell-like white, pink, blue and red flowers during summer and autumn.

Provide the plants with a humid atmosphere, keep them moist and feed with liquid manure weekly from the formation of buds until the last flower falls. As the leaves turn yellow, cease watering, gradually remove the dead flowers and leaves, remove the corms from the pot and store them in a dry place at 10°C (50°F). Re-start growth in early spring by plunging the plants into growing compost and placing in a propagator.

Gloxinias are either propagated from seed at a temperature of 15°C (60°F), or else they can be propagated from leaf cuttings.

There are few more colourful or easier to grow pot plants for greenhouses than *Senecio cruenta*.

## Stephanotis floribunda
## (Madagascar jasmine)

Stove. This evergreen, twining shrub has dark green leaves and heavily perfumed, white, waxy flowers from May to October.

It can be grown in large pots or in the greenhouse border, from either of which it is trained up wires or a cane framework. The best winter temperature is 13°C (55°F), but from April until late October it should not fall below 18°C (64°F) for long (a higher temperature does not matter). Keep the plant just moist in winter. While it is growing give ample water and maintain a humid atmosphere. Provide a little shade during the summer, otherwise let it have full light. Feed fortnightly with liquid manure from May to September.

Propagate from cuttings of lateral non-flowering shoots in a propagator at 18-21°C (64-70°F).

*Right:* Strelitzia is grown for its large, dramatic flowers.
*Below: Stephanotis floribunda* is an exquisite, sweetly scented climbing plant for greenhouses.

## Strelitzia
## (bird of paradise flower)

Stove. *Strelitzia reginae* is an evergreen, stove-house perennial that yields the most intriguing bird's-head-shaped flowers of green, purple, orange and blue in April and May.

In winter it needs a temperature of 10°C (50°F) and to be kept nearly dry. Water freely during spring and summer. Prevent scorching of the leaves by shading, and ventilate when necessary to lower the summer temperature to 18-21°F (64-70°F). Pot on or re-pot every second year in March. Liquid-feed fortnightly while growing.

Propagate by detaching single-rooted shoots after flowering and potting them up in growing compost. Strelitzia is also raised from seed which should be germinated at 18-21°C (64-70°F).

53

## Streptocarpus
## (cape primrose)

Cool or warm. These are showy hybrids with large, corrugated leaves and flowers of red, purple and white between May and October.

During winter streptocarpus requires a temperature of 10°C (50°F), and then 13°C (55°F). Water freely during the growing period and sparingly in winter. Shade the glass, and ventilate when necessary during the summer. Feed with weak liquid manure fortnightly from May to September. Propagate streptocarpus by division or leaf cuttings, or sow seeds.

## Tradescantia fluminensis

Cool or warm. This species has leaves that turn pale purple underneath in bright light.

*Below: Tradescantia fluminensis* 'Variegata are some of the most easily grown of greenhouse trailing plants.

*Above:* Streptocarpus hybrids are very popular greenhouse plants.

'Quicksilver' is a silver variegated variety. Tradescantia needs a winter temperature not lower than 7-10°C (45-50°F). The plant should be kept just moist. Water freely during the growing season. Position in good light, out of direct sunlight. Re-pot annually in April. Feed with weak liquid manure fortnightly from May to September.

This plant is easily propagated from tip cuttings at 16°C (61°F).

## Zantedeschia aethiopica (Arum lily)

Cool or warm. The arum lily has beautiful large white flowers with a conspicuous yellow spadix and large, green, slightly glossy arrow-shaped leaves. It flowers from March to June, according to the temperature in which it is kept.

The handsome, large, white flowers of *Zantedeschia aethiopica* are very useful for flower arranging.

*Z. elliottiana* is another lovely species, with yellow blooms and green leaves with silvery spots.

After flowering, the plants are dried off and rested with the pots lying on their sides. During August and September re-pot in a potting compost to which some bonemeal has been added. Stand the pots outdoors, water them well and bring them into the greenhouse in early October. When the roots are growing well, regularly feed with liquid manure. Spray the foliage against greenfly.

Arum lilies are propagated from offsets, which may be taken at the time of re-potting the plant.

# 11 Garden frames and cloches

Like greenhouses, garden frames and cloches give another dimension to gardening. Although the principle embodied is quite an old one, it remains very popular and is still being developed as a current technique. Frames and cloches have common functions, but there are marked differences in the manner in which they are used. They afford protection to plants of various types against adverse weather conditions and can extend their growing season.

## Garden frames

A garden frame is perhaps rather more complementary to a greenhouse than a cloche. There are, for example, many greenhouse subjects which can spend much of their time under a frame, and thus release space in the greenhouse. In fact, younger plants often flourish better in its cooler environment. Also, after flowering, plants can be transferred to a frame from the greenhouse to dry off and rest. A frame is essential for hardening off bedding plants, and for raising and propagating many types of plant. When no greenhouse is available, a garden frame can be heated by means of warming cables.

**Garden frame structure** Basically, frames have base walls made of tongued and grooved timber, metal, breeze blocks, plastic or sometimes glass, on the top of which is fixed a light which is a wooden or metal frame glazed with glass or PVC.

**Choosing garden frames** The frame's purpose will dictate what type should be bought. For raising seedlings, rooting cuttings and growing vegetables such as lettuce or early carrots, the frame need not be very high. The more usual lean-to type, with a height of 45cm (18in) at the back and 30cm (12in) at the front, will therefore

A traditional garden frame, constructed in timber and glass, is an invaluable adjunct to a greenhouse, but it also has its own particular functions.

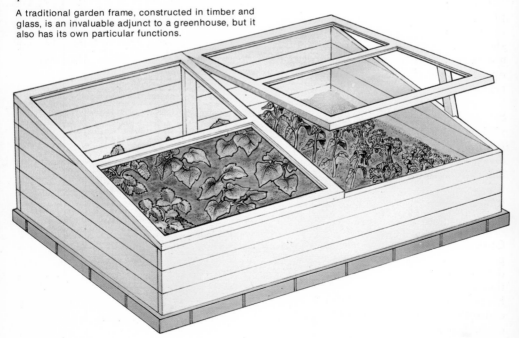

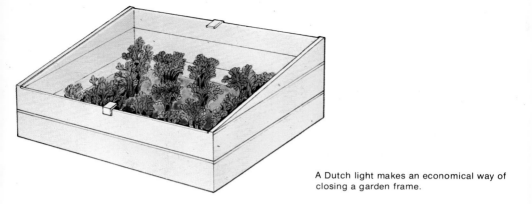

A Dutch light makes an economical way of closing a garden frame.

serve. This type is usually fitted at the top with a 2 x 1·25m (6 x 4ft) or 1·25 x 1·25m (4 x 4ft) light which slides up and down on runners. A cheaper and simpler form is the Dutch light, which is composed of a single sheet of glass 150 x 78cm (59 x 30in), held in a frame. The glass slides in rebates in the styles and is secured at the top and bottom by means of cleats.

For higher-growing plants, such as pot plants, French beans and cauliflowers, more depth is needed and a span-roof frame should be chosen. This is like a mini-greenhouse, with lights, that can be opened, sloping from the side walls to a central high ridge.

**Siting garden frames** The site should be well-drained, and not too near buildings or trees, which will deprive the frame of light and could be the cause of damage from falling debris. A wooden-base frame should be stood on a course of bricks. Lean-to frames are best placed against a wall facing south or south-west.

**Cleanliness and ventilation** It is important to keep frames free of rotting debris, and the glass clean. Good ventilation is essential when frames are in use. Both temperature and air ventilation are controlled by opening and closing the lights of the frames.

**Shading** Some form of shading, for example, a thin lime wash on the lights, should be provided during hot weather.

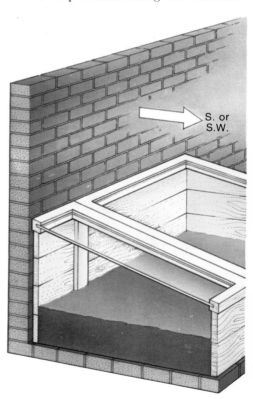

A lean-to frame should be positioned against a south- or southwest-facing wall.

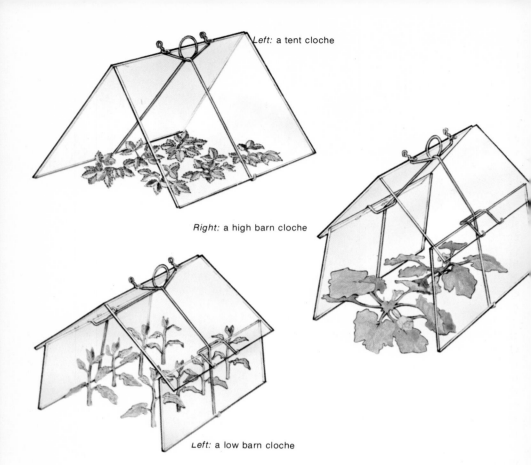

*Left:* a tent cloche

*Right:* a high barn cloche

*Left:* a low barn cloche

## Cloches

Although many of the functions of cloches, such as propagating, protecting plants against frost and producing early and tender growth, are similar to those of garden frames, the difference between them is that under cloches cultivation is carried on in the conventional manner – planting in continuous rows – whereas frames are used more as an extension of the greenhouse. Cloches are easily moved from one crop to another, and they provide easy access to crops at specific points.

**Choosing cloches** There are several types of cloche available. In glass, there are three main shapes. The tent cloche is com-

prised of two sheets of glass held firmly together by means of an inverted V-shaped wire, upturned at each end, on which the glass rests. The whole is held together by a

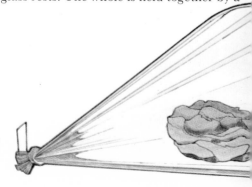

spring handle, which permits extra ventilation. The size when erected is 60cm (2ft) long x 30cm (1ft) wide x 25cm (10in) high.

The 'low barn' cloche is comprised of four sheets of glass which, by means of wire, form a cloche with two almost vertical sides at the base and a span roof. This type of cloche is 60cm (2ft) long x 57·5cm (23in) wide x 32·5cm (13in) high.

The 'high barn' cloche is similar to the last, except that it has taller sides, of 47·5cm (19in).

Plastic cloches usually take the form of a sheet of PVC inserted into hoops and secured with clips. Regular sizes are 45cm (18in) long x 30cm (1ft) wide x 25cm (10in) high; and 60cm (2ft) long x 30cm (1ft) x 22·5cm (9in) high. There are also models constructed in rigid plastic, needing no metal fittings but secured with pegs.

The three major advantages of plastic cloches are that they are lighter in weight, cheaper than glass, and unbreakable. On the other hand, they are less durable, they must be well secured or could blow away, they lose heat more rapidly at night, and condensation does not run down the sides as it does on glass, therefore light entry can be impeded.

Plastic continuous-tunnel cloche kits consist of polythene sheeting, supporting hoops and securing wires which erected, form a tunnel 9–11 m (30–35ft) long.

*Below:* The plastic tunnel, a more recent innovation, protects a row of plants as effectively as the older types of cloche and is more easily stored when not in use.

**Using cloches** Individual glass or plastic cloches should be placed end to end along each row of produce (early or more tender types of vegetables, fruit and flowers). The ends of the tunnel should be closed with glass or polythene sheets.

**Siting cloches** The site of the run must be away from buildings and trees so that no shadows are cast. Each cloche must be placed on previously prepared fertilised ground. The tunnel must be in place for a fortnight or so before sowing to warm up and dry out the soil so that a good tilth can be made and germination assisted.

**Cloche cultivation** Individual cloches can be moved aside easily at any specific point to provide access for weeding, spraying and so forth.

**Cleanliness and ventilation** Clean glass and plastic regularly. As the weather warms, the cloches should be opened

*Above:* A plastic cloche has the advantage over glass cloches of being unbreakable and less dangerous in gardens where young children play.

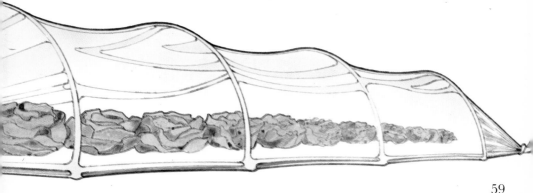

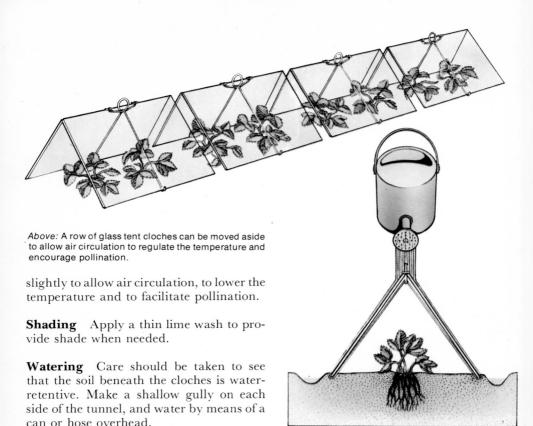

*Above:* A row of glass tent cloches can be moved aside to allow air circulation to regulate the temperature and encourage pollination.

slightly to allow air circulation, to lower the temperature and to facilitate pollination.

**Shading** Apply a thin lime wash to provide shade when needed.

**Watering** Care should be taken to see that the soil beneath the cloches is water-retentive. Make a shallow gully on each side of the tunnel, and water by means of a can or hose overhead.

**Plants for garden frames and cloches** Dates refer to the approximate harvesting or gathering time.

Plants under cloches are watered from overhead so that water flows into gullies on either side.

## Vegetables

Asparagus (March)
Aubergines
Dwarf French beans (mid-June)
Cabbage (February-March)
Capsicum
Carrots (May)
Celery (self-blanching)
    (early August)
Cucumbers
Endive
Lettuce (spring and winter)
Peas (early May)
Sweet corn
Tomatoes

## Fruit

Strawberries
Melon

## Flowers

Anemone (winter)
Calendula (late winter)
Gladioli
Dutch iris
Lily of the valley (April)
Brompton stocks (mid-April)
Violets (October)
Zinnias (early July)

60

# 12 Common greenhouse pests and diseases

In the tables below are described some of the troubles that affect greenhouse plants.

## Pests

| Pest | | Susceptible plants | Signs | Remedies |
|---|---|---|---|---|
| Aphids (greenfly) | | Most | Stems, leaves and buds are swarmed with green larvae. Young growth disfigured. | Spray with formathion or dimethoate. |
| Caterpillars | | All | Eaten or curled leaves. | Spray with trichlorphon or malathion. |
| Leaf hoppers | | Many | Coarse mottling on upper sides of leaves. | Regular fumigation of greenhouse with BHC. |
| Leaf miners | | Chrysanthemums, cinerarias and other pot plants | Leaves tunnelled. | Fumigate or spray with BHC. |
| Mealy bugs | | Many | Small tufts or waxy wool appearing on leaves and stems. | Spray with dimethoate or formathion |
| Red spider mites | | Many | Yellow mottling on upper side of leaves. Yellowing of leaves, then bronzing and ultimately leaf fall. | Regular fumigation with azobenzene. Spray with dimethoate. |
| Scale insects | | Many | Leaves and stems become sticky; closer examination shows that stems are covered with brown, yellow or white scales. | Spray with malathion or petroleum emulsion. |

61

| Pest | | Susceptible plants | Signs | Remedies |
|------|---|----------|-------|----------|
| Tarsonemid mites | | Many | Young shoots, leaves, etc., become distorted, discoloured and scarred. | No effective chemical control available, but sulphur dust or lime-sulphur sprays limit the infestation. |
| Thrips | | Various species attack many plants | Plants become covered with black flies. Distortion occurs. | Spray with malathion. |
| Weevils | | Begonias, cyclamen, vines pelargoniums, primulas, etc. | Plants collapse owing to roots being eaten. | Spray foliage with or add BHC, as a dust, to potting compost. |
| White flies | | Many | Underside of leaves infested with white scales, which are immature white flies. | Fumigate with BHC to kill the adults and spray the undersides of the leaves to kill the young. |

## Diseases

| Disease | Susceptible plants | Signs | Remedies |
|---------|----------|-------|----------|
| Blackroot-rot | Many | Rotting of the roots and tissues at the crown. Tissues become black. | Water plants with a solution of captan. |
| Bud drop | Camellias, stephanotis, etc. | Buds drop off before flowering. | Often caused by dry soil condition at bud formation; sometimes caused by extremes of day and night temperatures. |
| Carnation stem rot and die-back | Carnations | Stems rotting. | Control by spraying stock plants with captan a fortnight before and while taking cuttings. |
| Damping off | All seedlings and cuttings | Collapsing and dying. | Overcrowding, growing in too wet conditions, in compacted soil or in too high a temperature should be avoided. Check attacks by watering seed-boxes with captan. |
| Foot rot | Calceolaria, geraniums, etc. | Blackening and rotting at the base. | May be caused by contamination of water supply from a tank or butt. Add small pea-size lump of copper sulphate or crystals of potassium permanganate until water just pink, to purify. |

| Disease | Susceptible plants | Signs | Remedies |
|---|---|---|---|
| Grey mould (botrytis) | Most greenhouse plants | Greyish, velvety fungus on leaves, etc., with ultimate decay. | Remove and burn infected parts. Give good ventilation. Fumigate or dust the greenhouse with tecnazene or spray with captan or benomyl. |
| Gummosis | Cucumbers, melons | Distorted fruits, sunken spots, exuding gummy liquid, which becomes covered with dark green fungus. | Ventilate and heat adequately. Burn all infected fruits. Spray with zineb or captan. |
| Leafspot | Primulas, anthurium, dracaenas, etc. | Pale brown, irregular spots. | Remove dead leaves. Spray with captan, maneb or zineb. |
| Mildew, downy | Lettuce and other ornamental plants | White tufts or downy patches, usually on undersides of leaves. | Spray with thiram. |
| Mildew, powdery | Carnations, cucumbers, grapes, chrysanthemums, etc. | White powdery coating on stems and leaves. | Fumigate with dinocap. |
| Physiological disorders | Many plants | Brown and yellow blotches on leaves, browning of leaf tips, splitting of leaves, dropping leaves, etc. | Generally improve conditions. Give adequate watering; attend to nutriments, correct temperature, humidity levels, and so on. |
| Rust | Cineraria, carnations, beans, apricots | Brown or black spots on foliage. | Encouraged by high humidity which should be controlled by increasing ventilation; destroy leaves and badly infected plants. Spray with thiram and zineb. |
| Tomato leaf mould | Tomatoes | Yellow blotches on upper sides of leaves; purple-brown mould underneath. | Good cultivation and a maximum temperature of 21°C (70°F) usually prevent trouble. Also spray with zineb, or maneb. |
| Virus diseases | Tomatoes, strawberries, narcissi, chrysanthemums, cucumbers, carnations, etc. | Wide range of symptoms includes colour changes in leaves and stems and flowers, distortion, wilting, stunting of growth, etc. | Destroy any suspect and seedy plants for which there is no obvious explanation for ill-health. Virus disease is spread by common greenhouse pests, so always destroy them. |

# Index